STUDIES IN FRENCH LITERATURE No. 8

General Editor

W. G. Moore

Emeritus Fellow of St. John's College, Oxford

D1390679

FLAUBERT:
MADAME BOVARY

by

ALISON FAIRLIE

Professor of French and Fellow of Girton College, Cambridge

EDWARD ARNOLD

© *Alison Fairlie 1962*

First published 1962 by
Edward Arnold (Publishers) Ltd
25 Hill Street, London W1X 8LL

Reprinted 1965
Reprinted 1969
Reprinted 1973
Reprinted 1976

ISBN: 0 7131 5514 0

Printed in Great Britain by
The Camelot Press Ltd, Southampton

Contents

Introductory Note

Madame Bovary was written between 1851 and 1856. Its origins have been much discussed; they will be only briefly mentioned here, as a background to the study of the book itself.[1]

Maxime Du Camp recounted how, when he and Bouilhet had listened with consternation to Flaubert reading the first version of *La Tentation de Saint Antoine*, and told him it was unfit for publication, Bouilhet suggested that Flaubert should turn to a contemporary subject and write the story of the life and death of a local doctor's wife, Mme Delamare. Du Camp's evidence is far from reliable, and whatever germ of general truth there may be in this story, it has given rise to a great deal of suspect legend; much time has been spent in trying to decide which chemist was the original of Homais, or which exact village in Normandy was the model for Yonville, as well as on fragmentary and uncertain accounts of the life of Mme Delamare.

Two important articles by G. Leleu and J. Pommier (*Revue d'Histoire Littéraire de la France*, 1947) raised more substantial points. Flaubert had among his papers a manuscript narrative of the love-affairs and debts of Mme Pradier, who also talked to him at length about her woes (see the correspondence); she may well have contributed something to the creation of Emma. There is, however, a striking contrast between the atmosphere of the manuscript, with its flat narration and tone of prurient scorn, and Flaubert's way of treating Emma. Still more important (and stressed by M. Pommier) is the fact that Flaubert's letters show him, from very early in his career, constantly haunted by the theme of the aspiring and frustrated woman, so that he naturally and gradually makes use of very varied material to enrich different versions of it. Emma is not copied from any individual: certain details come from several women he knew closely, others from his reading, many from his critical insight into his own longings and his own weaknesses.

Certainly Flaubert used both direct experience and careful documentation (at a funeral he consciously set out to analyse the personal feelings that might be transposed into Charles Bovary; he attended an agricultural show; he studied medical technicalities and the reading of convent schoolgirls). But these details are used to give substance and form to themes that are already clearly outlined in his earliest unpublished works. The

[1] For fuller discussion, see especially the two works of C. Gothot-Mersch and the study by Cl. Digeon (cf. below, p. 80).

cold careerist and seducer, the futile romantic woman who dies of poison, were there in works written when he was sixteen (*Quidquid volueris* and *Passion et Vertu*); the Homais household is briefly prefigured in the grocer's family who so cheerfully discuss the hideous melodrama in one of these; Bournisien stems from an incident in *Agonies*, and the hero of *Mémoires d'un Fou* foretells Léon and Justin. By the time we come to *Novembre* and the first version of *L'Education sentimentale*, the themes, incidents and details that will be reshaped in *Madame Bovary* are legion.

The plans for *Madame Bovary*, published by J. Pommier and G. Leleu (Corti, 1949), show clearly that Flaubert does not start by copying individuals from real life, but patiently constructs the inner logic of an imagined character. He might use as grist to his mill any fact he met in his life or his reading, but the final principle is his own remark that the artist looks at many different people, 'les étudie, les compare et fait de tout cela une synthèse à son image'.[1]

1. Problems

Si j'ôte de la trivialité, j'ôterai de l'ampleur.   (*Corr.* III 20)

Je ne crois même pas que le romancier doive exprimer son opinion sur les choses de ce monde. Il peut la communiquer mais je n'aime pas . . . qu'il la dise.   (*Corr.* V 396)

The anti-heroic subject

When Baudelaire wrote a review of *Madame Bovary* on its publication in 1857 he called it 'ce livre essentiellement suggestif'.[2] This apparently simple story of a frustrated, passionate, pretentious provincial, her adulteries, her money muddles and her death, probes into all our preconceptions about the categories and values of human experience—sensuous, emotional, intellectual, moral or aesthetic. To read it with understanding is as much to investigate ourselves as to appreciate Flaubert. The particular mixture of admiration and exasperation which it has provoked

---

[1] (References are given to Book and Chapter for quotations from *Madame Bovary*. *Corr.* indicates the *Correspondance* in the Conard edition, and P.L. the extended early versions of the novel edited by Pommier and Leleu; for details see below, p. 80.)

[2] Pléiade edition of Baudelaire, pp. 1003–1013.

in sensitive and penetrating critics is in itself a measure of the richness and stimulus of its suggestions.

The main character of this book is no 'heroine': she is to be different from the 'fastueuses bavardes de l'époque qui nous a précédés'.[1] In the first half of the nineteenth century the hero was often the hypersensitive and frustrated genius, claiming unalloyed sympathy and admiration. And if sensibility and suffering were to be stressed, woman, tied by convention or circumstance, was a particularly likely symbol. Madame de Staël's *Delphine* and *Corinne*, George Sand's *Indiana* and *Lélia*, with all their moments of intelligent analysis, yet show heroines who trail a high and grandiloquent anguish through picturesque exotic landscapes or civilised salons. The character, the background and the very name of Emma Bovary bring us down to earth.

Through the centuries, periods of heroic or sentimental literature have been followed by works of puncturing parody or earthy contrast. The theme of a deluded character naïvely attempting to apply in the world as it is the dreams inherited from works of fiction has flourished in many countries at different times: the greatest masterpiece it produced, Cervantes' *Don Quixote*, Flaubert said he knew almost by heart even before he could read for himself. Rabelais too started from the parody of a chronicle of giants, and Flaubert at the age of sixteen longed to be a nineteenth-century Rabelais, directing great gusts of healthy laughter at the follies of his times and of himself. If it is in works like *La Tentation de Saint Antoine* or *Bouvard et Pécuchet* that his love of fantastic imagination or biting caricature will be fully indulged, yet even in *Madame Bovary* there is a strain of deliberate parody woven into the everyday detail that so rigorously refuses his adulterous heroine any vestige of grandiose circumstance; the headlong course of the cab through Rouen in Book III is rabelaisian in its extravagance and its elaborations, and the whole Homais family is joyously and justifiably more than life-size in its satire on contemporary reality.

In the nineteenth century a reaction by serious novelists against sentimental idealism and exoticism was bound to come, and *Madame Bovary* was certainly not its first sign. Baudelaire's article points out that the public of the 1850s had grown weary and suspicious of noble and poetic subjects and demanded 'realism', mistakenly imagining that this vague and much misused word implied an unselective copy of the superficial

[1] ibid., p. 1008.

details of everyday life. Flaubert of course always refused to be classed with the group who called themselves 'realists' in his day, and never thought of art as a mere 'copy of reality'.

> La Réalité, selon moi, ne doit être qu'un tremplin. Nos amis sont persuadés qu'à elle seule elle constitue tout l'Art (*Corr. Supp.* IV 52).

Differing uses of the words 'real', 'reality' and 'realistic' have unfortunately made 'realism', both in the nineteenth century and since, an ill-defined critical term. There are after all as many angles of vision on reality as there are human beings; aspects of the reality of a tree may be seen by an atomic physicist, a farm labourer or an impressionist painter. And any representation of reality is of necessity selective: the attempt to give every detail of the objects in one small room might extend to infinity. Realism is no more than one kind of technique for selectively representing one way of looking at reality; it reacts against previous traditions which chose the fantastic, the idealistic or the exceptional, and sets out to create the illusion of observing impartially the ordinary events of average life. It need not logically imply insistence on the sordid, though in reacting against abstract and idealised presentations it may come to stress this side of things. A great writer within a roughly realistic tradition will study and use the facts and objects of everyday life, but will be well aware that his work is no exact copy. Flaubert constantly insisted that to produce the illusion of reality one must select and heighten detail and fit it to a satisfying pattern:

> On ne peut faire vrai qu'en choisissant et en exagérant . . . exagérer harmonieusement (*Corr. Supp.* II 118).[1]

The great artist of the 1850s, Baudelaire's article remarked, will choose what the public has come to want—the most commonplace subject from daily life—choose it not to copy superficially but to show what new possibilities it holds. What is the most petty and uninteresting background?—the small town in the provinces; what the most stereotyped barrel-organ theme churned out through the ages?—adultery. It is these apparently unpromising materials which will be transformed by precision and subtlety of expression, strength and seriousness of meaning.

[1] Several articles and books have pointed out contradictions in details and impossibilities in time-scheme in the novel. These would be noticed only by the most attentive reader. Flaubert must have overlooked them because atmosphere counted for more than accuracy.

In 1829 Hugo had already insisted 'Il n'y a ni bons ni mauvais sujets, mais de bons et de mauvais poètes', and the whole nineteenth century was discovering that, in Baudelaire's words on *Madame Bovary*, 'tous les sujets sont indifféremment bons ou mauvais, et . . . les plus vulgaires peuvent devenir les meilleurs.' The novel was in any case less hidebound by noble conventions than poetry. Many lesser novelists were turning to everyday subjects, and meeting the perennial difficulty of making them significant without false dramatisation, authentic without dullness or disorder. Each great writer finds a different solution. Before Flaubert, both Balzac and Stendhal had turned to the rich triviality of contemporary life. But their central characters are still outstanding individuals, whether in intelligence, sensitivity, villainy or sheer force of resistance, and they usually lead eventful lives, forging their way upwards with relentless persistence or meeting a downfall paradoxically satisfying in the very intensity of its drama. Flaubert allows no such outlet.

Originally he wished to write the story of a poor girl who wasted away her life among the cabbages and fruit-trees of a provincial garden and to whom nothing whatever happened.[1] The author who thinks previous stylisations have misrepresented life is often drawn to this removal of 'plot', and modern theorists of the 'anti-roman' have many predecessors. Flaubert with his sense of how the dream never fits reality is particularly fascinated by the idea of anatomising the dream in a complete void. In *Saint Antoine* he does this, but his friends had rejected the first version of *Saint Antoine*. Emma is allowed the at least potentially dramatic experiences of marriage, two lovers and suicide. But her husband is inept and cloddish, her lovers prosaically practical and pettily pusillanimous. She would have been in her element facing the vengeful passion of the Brazilian Baron from *La Cousine Bette* or even the clumsy pistol-shot of Julien Sorel in *Le Rouge et le Noir*; whereas, when she fears her husband may appear and cries anxiously to her lover 'As-tu tes pistolets?', Rodolphe greets her question with blank incomprehension and amused scorn. Her momentary experience of longed-for luxury, which haunts her for the rest of her life, consists of one night at a country-house ball where the owners are condescendingly entertaining some of the local electors. In his plans Flaubert had thought of a visit to Paris, but the book concentrates the claustrophobic atmosphere and Emma never escapes further than the few miles to Rouen. The threat of discovery is represented by a neighbour out duck-shooting, crouched on a

[1] *Corr.* II 253; IV 169.

muddy path behind an old barrel, or by the need to forge a bill for piano lessons from a Rouen spinster. As for her suicide, it is determined not simply by love but by financial muddle, the bailiffs at the door and the insufferable thought of Charles' inevitable patience: she dies not of a wasting disease, but in the full unpleasant detail of vomiting and emetics.

When Balzac takes outwardly insignificant characters, he uses every resource of image, analogy and intensification to magnify their scale, until an abbé Troubert in the provinces takes on the scope, stature and menace of medieval Pope or Emperor. The actions of the most apparently petty individual are made to affect a vast social network, and even the meek victims, shut away from a wider society, an Eugénie Grandet or a Mme de Mortsauf, have their own kind of inflexible grandeur. Stendhal may direct irony and criticism at his heroes, but he involves them in great events and regards them basically with amused but decided admiration. Both in choice of events and in presentation of character Flaubert subjects his actors to what Baudelaire called his 'dureté systématique'.

From Sainte-Beuve onwards there have been critics who wished the novel might have had one main character whom the reader could whole-heartedly admire. But Flaubert deliberately set out to render impossible any comfortably easy judgment on human affairs.

> Le plus haut dans l'art [he wrote], et le plus difficile, ce n'est ni de faire rire, ni de faire pleurer, mais de faire rêver (*Corr.* III 322).

This expression, 'faire rêver', stands for two of his most deeply ingrained reactions. The first is an intellectual sense of the contrasts, complexities and paradoxes that make it impossible to sum up human behaviour in facile categories of good or evil, pettiness or nobility:

> Que je sois pendu si je porte jamais un jugement sur qui que ce soit! La bêtise n'est pas d'un côté et l'esprit de l'autre. C'est comme le vice et la vertu; malin qui les distingue (*Corr.* IV 83)

What exasperates him in the bourgeois is not principally vulgarity or plain stupidity, but the bland, self-satisfied, unquestioning certainty that confines complex human experience in tabloid maxims and deforming platitudes. At the centre of his construction of characters is the basic conjunction 'but . . .'—Emma aspiring but affected, Charles devoted but insupportable. Then, besides the intellectual desire to provoke conflicting reflections, there is in Flaubert a kind of sheer marvelling stupefaction before the richness and strangeness of things as they are. 'Tout me fait rêver . . . Pour qu'une chose soit intéressante, il suffit de la regarder longtemps' (*Corr.* I 192). There is no need to magnify the person or object, to endow it with discrepant or spurious dignity: the mind of the artist will patiently penetrate, as it contemplates the humblest thing, its individual and suggestive value. Maupassant tells how Flaubert held that

> Il y a dans tout de l'inexploré, parce que nous sommes habitués à ne nous servir de nos yeux qu'avec le souvenir de ce qu'on a pensé avant nous . . . La moindre chose contient un peu d'inconnu. Trouvons-le.

Baudelaire in his notebooks spoke of moments when 'la profondeur de la vie se révèle dans l'objet, si ordinaire qu'il soit, que l'on a sous les yeux'; Flaubert saw the ridiculous cap of the schoolboy Charles as holding 'des profondeurs d'expression comme le visage d'un imbécile'. To contemplate 'le visage d'un imbécile' may suggest reflections about the nature of things which allows it to exist, about the gap which separates it from the 'normal' or 'superior' intelligence, and about the disturbing parallels through which it is related to that intelligence, echoes it or shows something about its processes. In Flaubert's creation of characters who are deliberately limited, if in no literal sense idiots, there is the same threefold stimulus: a questioning of destiny and a constant and very individual shift between involvement and detachment.

This is a book which combines parody, representation and poetry in a particularly original way. Baudelaire remarked that here 'les paroles les plus solennelles sortiront des bouches les plus sottes'. Two great artists, Henry James and Paul Valéry, have expressed doubts about this way of creating characters. Valéry, who prefers *Saint Antoine*, considers that Emma's range of sensibility is inadequate as an instrument to convey the vision of life that Flaubert has to suggest; Henry James, while he deeply admires the book, thinks Emma shows, though to a lesser extent, the same artistic flaw as he finds in Frédéric of *L'Education sentimentale:* these characters lack the dignity and representative value that would make them satisfactory 'reflectors and registers' of human experience. The problem is vital: it is only by the end of this brief study that I hope to outline other possible ways of looking at it. Yet it might be suggested from the start that an author may convey vision and values not simply by reflection in his characters but by refraction from them, not always through their range of consciousness but in their most inarticulate urges and apprehensions.

The art of insinuation

No one is likely today to see *Madame Bovary* as the prosecution presented it in 1857: a dangerous and corrupting inducement to adultery. Already Henry James enjoyed pointing out that it might equally well serve as a Sunday-school tract on the opposite side. To Flaubert himself the writer's business is to create the illusion of life and leave the reader to draw his own conclusions:

> Si le lecteur ne tire pas d'un livre la moralité qui doit s'y trouver, c'est que le lecteur est un imbécile ou que le livre est *faux* au point de vue de l'exactitude ... Les livres obscènes ne sont même immoraux que parce qu'ils manquent de vérité (*Corr.* VII 285).

The book shocked some contemporaries for two reasons: first because it expressed with sharp and sensuous precision of detail, and set in a familiar background, things they were accustomed to see in more abstract and lofty terms; then, because it did not draw a moral explicitly. Here we come to the central problem in Flaubert's way of treating his subject: one that has sometimes been over-simplified.

'De glace ... objectif, impersonnel'—so Baudelaire defined the tone of the narrator in *Madame Bovary*. Clearly in any author the impression of impartiality is a purely relative matter, or an illusion: absolute objectivity is impossible. Proust was even to point out the paradox that in a novel the apparently objective statement: 'elle était bien gentille' implies a sharing of personal judgments about what is likeable, whereas the subjective form 'J'avais du plaisir à l'embrasser' is a factual statement. The author will always, whether intentionally or not, imply a personal angle of vision: but there are many different tones he may choose to adopt. Flaubert stated his intentions as 'Nul lyrisme, pas de réflexions, personnalité de l'auteur absente' (*Corr.* II 361). Many of his early works had been self-analyses where criticism of the author-hero was outweighed by sympathy for him; he wants now to avoid any complicity between author, characters and reader. Of course he is aware of how much of himself there is in his works: when he writes firmly 'plus vous serez personnel, plus vous serez faible', he immediately adds: 'j'ai toujours péché par là, moi, je me suis toujours mis dans tout ce que j'ai fait' (*Corr.* II 461), and,

> le cœur que j'étudiais, c'était le mien. *Bovary* n'aura une valeur originale que par ce côté (*Corr.* II 457).

But for an author to use the possibilities of his own nature in creating characters who are made individual and presented critically (all the more critically because each develops a facet of the writer's own personality) is very different from directly expressing personal feelings or judgments. Of *Madame Bovary* he writes uncompromisingly:

> Je veux qu'il n'y ait pas dans mon livre . . . *une seule* réflection de l'auteur (*Corr.* II 365).

Certainly he does not expansively confide his views like Balzac, nor interject the gaily or bitterly ironical comments of Stendhal. But it is often wrongly assumed that he never directly intervenes. The reader who decides to search the story for those moments when the author does suddenly and openly reflect in his own terms on human experience, relating his characters to what is felt by 'nous', 'vous', 'on', will be surprised by his discoveries, and will find that these unexpected asides, all the more important for their relative scarcity, penetrate to the quick of what Flaubert has to convey. But they are rare, and go against Flaubert's declared intentions; what is more immediately important in approaching *Madame Bovary* is to be alert to the art of insinuation.

Sometimes the issue is quite straightforward: the machinations of Lheureux or the pomposities and platitudes of Homais speak for themselves. The problem for author and reader is different at moments when the reader might be temped to identify himself with the central characters. When Flaubert is working on the chapter where Emma first meets Léon, he writes in a letter:

> Je suis à faire une conversation d'un jeune homme et d'une jeune dame sur la littérature, la mer, les montagnes, la musique, tous les sujets poétiques enfin. On pourrait la prendre au sérieux, et elle est d'une grande intention de grotesque. Ce sera, je crois, la première fois qu'on verra un livre qui se moque de sa jeune première et de son jeune premier (*Corr.* III 42-3).

Often it is by means of an image that he suggests or punctures: Charles going patiently about his daily tasks is compared to the blinkered horse that plods uncomprehendingly round the endless circle of the corn-mill, or Emma's dreams are likened to the white pigeons whose delicate feet dabble in the gutters of the inn. One outstanding sentence is worth looking at closely. Flaubert is evoking Charles' marvelling delight in the early days of his marriage: in the first phrases the suggestions of each physical detail of the countryside combine with the balance and gradual expansion of the rhythm to involve us in an experience of spreading tenderness, rich fulfilment, peace and shelter, warmth and vigour:

> Et alors, sur la grande route qui étendait sans en finir son long ruban de poussière, par les chemins creux où les arbres se courbaient en berceaux, dans les sentiers dont les blés lui montaient jusqu'aux genoux, avec le soleil sur les épaules et l'air du matin à ses narines, . . . il s'en allait . . .

then we are made to thud back to a sense of down-to-earth crudity in an almost brutish happiness:

> il s'en allait ruminant son bonheur, comme ceux qui mâchent encore, après dîner, le goût des truffes qu'ils digèrent (I 5).

Sometimes the puncturing works through a single word (the carriage which 'ressemblait *presque* à un tilbury'), sometimes through the sudden fierce discrepancy created by ironical juxtaposition of detail. We see the full bitterness of Emma's feeling of frustrating monotony; as she sits by the window her eye lights on the barber's shop. 'Lui aussi, le perruquier, il se lamentait de sa vocation arrêtée, de son avenir perdu'—would-be delicate aspirations are caricaturally echoed by the barber's desire for a more profitable and fashionable business.

There are other kinds of ironical incongruity—those within character. Whereas in an early version of one of the scenes analysing Emma's discontent (P.L. 298) Flaubert gives a direct judgment in general terms: 'elle se passionnait pour une chose sérieuse aussi bien qu'une futile', in the novel itself he leaves the implications to the reader, and simply presents the objects of her irritation in a sentence where ironically balanced phrases clamp together the wildly discrepant elements of her confused thinking:

> elle s'irritait d'un plat mal servi ou d'une porte entre-bâillée, gémissait du velours qu'elle n'avait pas, du bonheur qui lui manquait, de ses rêves trop hauts, de sa maison trop étroite (II 5).

But it is in the interplay between characters that Flaubert can set going his most stimulating suggestions. Two key scenes may serve as brief examples. When Emma and Léon first meet (II 2), three kinds of irony come into play. There is the contrapuntal criss-crossing of two sets of platitudes as Homais dissertates pretentiously on the advantages of the locality while Emma and Léon drift into flat clichés on sunsets, seascapes, music and literature. There is the comic clash between the conviction, cherished by both sides, that they are superior to the ordinary mortal, and the triteness or inadequacy of what they actually say. And there is the fact that ideas and expression are completely at odds: Homais describing the life of a country practitioner or the local climate decks them out in the resounding pontifical phraseology of 'où se heurteront quotidiennement les efforts de votre science' or 'engendrer des miasmes insalubres', while Léon, wanting to convey poetically the majesty of the mountains, can manage no more than the second-hand account by a cousin who once visited Switzerland, couched in the most vague and obvious terms: 'on ne peut se figurer la *poésie* des lacs, le *charme* des cascades, l'effet *gigantesque* des glaciers'.

Each slightest remark serves both to draw Emma and Léon together and to define their characters. Both feel restless, sensitive and superior, long for the Opera, Paris and the infinite in one heterogeneous amalgam, look in literature for emotional and self-congratulatory pleasure; yet already they are differentiated and their whole future in Book III is implied, for Léon, the more moderate, timorous and indecisive, prefers verse, tenderness and tears, while Emma, passionate, active, already imagining herself disillusioned and pushing always to extremes, has found poetry insufficient to her needs and turned to the intensified stimulus of tales of drama and terror.

The climax of comic deflation is reached as we see Léon adding to the mountain-tops the obligatory sentimental associations of prayer and ecstasy, culminating in the ridiculous anecdote of the famous musician who would whip up his imagination by transporting his piano to some imposing site. And in the background to this would-be passion and poetry the trivial world obtrudes as the incompetent and inappropriately named inn-servant Artémise slops in and out in her list slippers, forgetting the plates and leaving the door-latch to clatter against the wall.

Yet we are not left simply in critical detachment. As the scene goes on, Flaubert first conveys the sense of physical closeness drawing the two together, then broadens momentarily into the sentence that involves our own experience with that of the characters:

> ils entrèrent dans une de ces vagues conversations où le hasard des phrases vous ramène toujours au centre fixe d'une sympathie commune.

Anyone may have known that sudden sense of combined excitement and comfort as two human beings set out to explore what draws them to each other. Flaubert suggests troublous reflections around it through

B

characters who are a mixture of vague but genuine need (shown both physically and mentally), self-deceiving affectation and sheer incapacity to find words that will ever adequately shape their feelings.

One other scene shows specially clearly the problems that faced Flaubert, and the many-sided suggestions he creates: Emma's visit to the curé Bournisien (II 6). There are only two characters here, but they are playing a quartet of implications.

Emma in a state of confused desperation goes to the priest; he is preoccupied with the affairs of others and with the catechism-class, hardly hears what she is saying, and attributes her suffering to physical causes—the heat or indigestion. A similar incident in one of Flaubert's early works[1] had made a sentimentally simplified contrast between the hero, nobly in despair at the world and himself, and the crude priest with his mind set on whether his potatoes were boiling over. In *Madame Bovary* the effect is much more subtle. Two characters are set at cross-purposes; each is shown as in part genuine, in part pretentious and imperceptive, and behind them a wider problem is suggested.

In his correspondence, discussing the difficulty of conveying what he means 'sans une réflexion ni une analyse (tout en dialogue direct),' Flaubert outlines his intentions:

> Mon curé est très brave homme, excellent même . . . pratique tous ses devoirs . . . mais il ne songe qu'au physique (aux souffrances des pauvres, manque de pain ou de bois), et ne devine pas les défaillances morales, les vagues aspirations mystiques (*Corr.* III 166).

In the book, dialogue alone must convey these different sides. Bournisien's faults are made abundantly obvious—his language is studded with clerical clichés, heavy puns and complacent reference to the condescension of the bishop, and each vague but desperate attempt Emma makes to express her needs is met by an automatic return to physical explanations. But this is not a mind set on its own supper; if he keeps interrupting to rush off and cuff the catechism-class it is because he is plodding conscientiously on with an immediate task, unable to see beyond it; if the reference to 'une vache qui avait *l'enfle*' falls with grim incongruity after the phraseology on 'médecin des âmes', it is part of the picture of his practical place in village life, and if he waxes sentimental over the 'pauvres mères de famille, . . . de véritables saintes', he is at least theoretically aware of the problem of poverty which Emma loftily

---

[1] *Agonies*, in *Œuvres de Jeunesse inédites*, I, 411.

sweeps aside. The scene ends with the parrot-repetition of 'Qu'est-ce qu'un chrétien? . . . celui qui étant baptisé, baptisé, baptisé . . .', the mechanical formula handed on by the man of well-meaning ineptitude, and the implications are made the more bitter for his utterly limited good intentions, but Bournisien is not a flat caricature.

As for Emma, she has come to the Church not with any clear intention, but impelled by the almost somnambulistic impulse of sensuous memories from her convent days, called up by the Angelus, and by a longing to lose her torment in some ill-defined, all-embracing experience. Besides, the unrecognised source of her distress is that Léon is too timid to declare his love. She too falls into high-sounding cliché—'ce ne sont pas les remèdes de la terre qu'il me faudrait'; above all, her sentences can express no more than the negative—'my husband is no help; no, that is not what is wrong; what of those who have not . . .?'—for she cannot give positive form to her need. Scornfully she brushes aside the thought of her husband with the one word 'Lui!' and the deprivations of the poor with 'Eh! qu'importe?', as Bournisien replies with his equally sweeping conviction that to have fire and food is enough. Emma is muddled, affected, selfish and inarticulate, but she feels the need for something she cannot define and she genuinely suffers—a few bare phrases of physical description convey this: 'Elle fixa sur le prêtre des yeux suppliants', 'Et les coins de sa bouche se tordaient en parlant.' A scene that stringently shows up the posturings and inadequacies of both characters allows moments of understanding for each and calls up in the background the conflict and the relationship between man's physical needs and his less definable desires.

These are scenes of direct dialogue. An author who wishes to give the illusion of not intervening in his work will describe the actions, appearance, words and perhaps thoughts of his characters, but avoid pronouncing in abstract summary on their nature or their motives. Flaubert does sometimes make this kind of pronouncement—Emma is 'de tempérament plus sentimentale qu'artiste'; Léon abstains from excesses 'autant par pusillanimité que par délicatesse'. At other times he speaks as if considering alternative possibilities about an existing person—'Elle fit semblant de croire, ou crut-elle peut-être', or 'Etait-ce sérieusement qu'elle parlait ainsi? Sans doute qu'Emma n'en savait rien elle-même', underlining in this way the difficulty of judging motive. Normally he leaves descriptions, actions or thoughts to carry their own suggestions, implicit in context or expression.

Flaubert often mentioned in letters the infuriating problem of how to convey the mediocrity and banality of everyday speech, or the drift of half-formulated thought, and yet achieve a sharp and evocative effect. He succeeds often through the choice and concentration of platitudes set in the varied contexts of speech, letter or newspaper, and fitted acutely and aptly into individual situations. This is the surface of human relationships; more difficult to indicate is what lies beneath it.

In reporting thoughts, Flaubert moves between the direct form—'N'aime-t-il pas? se demanda-t-elle'—and the famous *style indirect libre*. He is probably the first to use this extensively in the French novel and in several ways it particularly suits the angles of vision he wishes to give. When Emma's meditations open: 'Comment avait-elle donc fait, elle qui était si intelligente . . .' the *était* is obviously no outside statement of fact about her, but an ironical measure of her illusions about herself. Then, the very fact that the same tense, the imperfect, serves for reporting thoughts and for describing real background makes for a world where illusion and reality interweave particularly closely. And, perhaps most important, this technique helps to solve the problem of how to convey with savour and precision the experience of characters who have themselves little command over words, for the author can move almost imperceptibly between their semi-inarticulate conceptions and his own more exact and heightened expression of them.

Emma could not herself have voiced her dreams with the excitement or nostalgia Flaubert's indirect expression gives them ('s'en aller vers ces pays à noms sonores où les lendemains de mariage ont de plus suaves paresses . . .' and the succeeding passage in I 7). Nor could she have summed up her disillusion and disgust in such physically evocative or rhythmically echoing phrases ('D'où venait donc cette insuffisance de la vie, cette pourriture instantanée des choses où elle s'appuyait . . .' and the continuation in III 6). At the same time the indirect summary can be one of the most telling ways of caricaturing without comment the tawdry or ridiculous content of her dreams and desires:

> Que ne pouvait-elle s'accouder sur le balcon des chalets suisses ou enfermer sa tristesse dans un cottage écossais, avec un mari vêtu d'un habit de velours à longues basques, et qui porte des bottes molles, un chapeau pointu et des manchettes (I 7—here the shift from imperfect to present tense both shows the growing strength of her illusion and ironically puts us closest to her thought at the very moment when its content sets us at a distance).

Flaubert has sometimes been accused of crowding his book with loving enumerations of mere objects; but to him the fascination lies in what the object reveals about the human mind, whether that mind created it, enjoys it, neglects or falsifies it. Emma's wedding-cake evokes the pretentious sentimentality of a whole social background. Places are seen not as an immutable essence but through the eyes of a given character, under the influence of a particular mood. In his plans he says about Yonville:

Le présenter d'abord comme un endroit assez agréable. Emma s'y plaît au commencement—puis comme atroce d'ennui aux époques où elle l'exècre (P.L. 15).

Sometimes we see simply what the characters are conscious of, sometimes their illusions as to what it is like, sometimes what affects them without their knowing it. Every detail depends on its context: when Emma sings to Léon as they go boating, Flaubert had originally described her voice as 'chevrotante et maigre'; in the final version he presents it not in his own words but as it would seem to the entranced Léon: 'harmonieuse et faible'.

Flaubert insisted that 'content' and 'form' are inextricably interdependent. In the present short study it has seemed preferable to comment on details of expression as they arise in their context rather than in a separate and systematic analysis. One or two very brief remarks here may suggest other general problems which the reader will want to think out personally.

Some critics, perhaps preferring the cultivated negligence of Stendhal, perhaps in keeping with the recent interest in a 'style neutre' or a 'degré zéro de l'écriture', have tended to see in Flaubert's style an over-conscious mosaic of 'devices'. Certainly this is a way of writing where language is not meant to appear simply a transparent vehicle for content, but to be a source of enjoyment in its own right. It is rich and deliberate (sometimes over-deliberate); it is also varied and flexible. Charles Du Bos remarked that it is a style which gives one a feeling of rarely coming up for air, yet that one is held by its unrivalled capacity to convey atmospheres and obsessions. Purists find it sometimes imprecise or awkward when Flaubert is grappling with the abstract analysis of mental processes: this reflects his sense of the fluid and uncertain elements in experience which must not be falsely simplified. Where he is most successful is of course in creating moods through the tiny details of the physical world.

Flaubert echoes and intensifies his meaning by balanced rhythm (particularly the 'ternary sentence' with developed crescendo or diminuendo), onomatopoeia and image. A writer who feels particularly strongly the difficulty of making language both precise and evocative is likely to be drawn to images as an allusive way of translating the indefinable. Flaubert, who noted wryly that in his initial versions images seemed to hop through his sentences as irrepressibly as fleas, removed many that were inapposite or merely decorative. Occasionally there remain some that appear strained or inappropriate (feelings shrivelling up like the body of the Duke of Clarence in the butt of wine),[1] but more often they use the objects of the characters' everyday experience to create parallels between physical and mental worlds, giving a new sharpness of sensation and power of suggestion.

Precise and subtle sense-impressions are used to evoke widely varied atmospheres and events: the stiff and bristling awkwardness of the guests at the village wedding; the soft and cloying scents and the hesitant or muffled sounds of a late summer evening; the horror of the gangrene that follows a bungled operation; the sights and smells of the narrow streets in Rouen that stifle Charles and stimulate Emma—or simply the sound of a rope trailing through the water, in a sentence where the choice and placing of every word is vital to the haunting effect:

> tandis qu'à l'arrière la bauce qui traînait ne discontinuait pas son petit clapotement doux dans l'eau (III 4).

Scents evoke a whole background: the smell of tar in Rouen docks, the aroma of incense from the wax-spotted Church chairs at the *Comices*, or the 'odeur d'iris et de draps humides' from the cupboard in the Rouault kitchen. Other sensations give the sudden impact of surroundings on a character: on her arrival by night at the empty house in Yonville, Emma (in a sentence where the postponement, the simile and the two hard monosyllables intensify the shock) 'dès le vestibule sentit tomber sur ses épaules, comme un linge humide, le froid du plâtre'.

Above all, Flaubert can convey the quality of light playing at odd angles on the texture of surfaces, as with the lamplight that strikes

---

[1] There are at times clumsy expressions ('tout ce qui ne contribuait pas à la consommation immédiate de son cœur', over-developed or inapt comparisons (Rodophe's heart like a playground trampled by schoolboys) and distortions of syntax. L. Bopp's *Commentaire sur Madame Bovary* gives many examples, some justified, some not.

horizontally on the pictures at La Vaubyessard ('elle se brisait contre elles en *arêtes fines*, selon les craquelures du vernis'), the shaft that touches the ashes in the kitchen fireplace ('le jour qui descendait par la cheminée, *veloutant* la suie de la plaque, *bleuissait* un peu les cendres froides'), or the oil patches on the river at sunset with sound and rhythm of words adding to their heavy drift, shifting shapes, and burnished gleam ('de larges gouttes grasses, ondulant inégalement sous la pourpre du soleil, comme des plaques de bronze florentin, qui flottaient').

Apart from the developed passages of sensuous elaboration, there is the skill in deliberately rapid narrative (Charles' early life, or the conclusion), and the swift, pungent satire, standing out in the conscious virtuosity of epigram: the opera-singer who 'tenait en même temps du coiffeur et du toréador', or Léon who, when with Emma, 'adorait en même temps l'élévation de son âme et les dentelles de sa jupe'. Each character is given his own style of speech; this is seen at its heights in Homais, but is equally worth savouring in le père Rouault's kindly meanderings or in the scolding reproaches of Charles' first wife and his mother ('Ce n'est pas la peine de faire tant de fla-fla'). Here again Flaubert does not give an exact representation of spoken speech, but exercises a conscious stylisation. He is aware of the challenge of 'faire du dialogue qui soit bien écrit': on the one hand he avoids the boredom of extended and inexpressive triviality by picking out a few telling expressions ('il y a du grabuge là-dessous' sums up Lheureux's suspicions of Emma), on the other, he removes for example from the first versions the over-coarse colloquialisms of Rodolphe yet in less startling words still conveys crudity of mind and language.[1]

At the opposite extreme from the precision of sensuous or intellectual observation is the art of suggesting almost indefinable states of mind: the utter emptiness of melancholy and monotony; the sudden surge of total satisfaction; or the obsessive desire to lose one's identity by being completely absorbed into something outside the self—another being, the natural universe, the city, religion or death. Finally there is the conveying of states of hysteria or semi-hallucination as in Emma's successive breakdowns or her last stupefied rush from Rodolphe's house when

> tout ce qu'il y avait dans sa tête de réminiscences, d'idées, s'échappait à la fois, d'un seul bond, comme les mille pièces d'un feu d'artifice ... Il lui sembla tout à coup que des globules couleur de feu éclataien

[1] See M. J. Durry: *Flaubert et ses Projets inédits*, p. 35.

dans l'air comme des balles fulminantes en s'aplatissant, et tournaient, tournaient (III 8).

But it is time to see these details in their setting. Flaubert himself constantly insisted that it is the thread which makes a necklace out of individual pearls, and, precisely because of his passionate contemplation of the tiniest object, he laid all the more stress on the importance of the art of construction.

2. Structure

Dans la précision des assemblages, . . . l'harmonie de l'ensemble, n'y a-t-il pas une vertu intrinsèque?   (Corr. VII 294)

Probably no novel has ever been so carefully planned. It has been called (with an undertone of condescension) a great feat of literary engineering; obviously it is very different from the unpruned and compelling exuberance of a Balzac, or from Stendhal's deliberately created impression of episodic and impromptu story-telling. This is not the art which hides art; it is the epitome of the visible and satisfying control of the human mind over its material, planning an architectural structure where the main outlines are boldly balanced and every detail is fitted to several purposes. Each time the novel is re-read, new echoes and undertones both add to our delight in significant pattern and suggest Flaubert's full awareness of the complexity of human substance.

One of the first things we notice is probably the careful placing of key points in story or in revelation of character; the inventive and rich use of simple incidents once they are fitted into their place. We are shown Emma's years as a convent schoolgirl (I 6) only when we have watched her for some time through the eyes of Charles and seen her married. This is the moment to pause and look into her past; it is also the moment when disillusionment would fittingly make Emma herself turn back to her early dreams. Much later, the death of Charles' father occurs at just the point when Emma returns in a kind of exultant stupor after giving in to Léon in Rouen: this offers many opportunities, first in the scene where

Homais breaks the news to her (III 2), then in the accident which shows her the poison she will later use, and finally in the dinner where she sits, half-lost in her passion, yet trying 'par savoir-vivre' to say the right thing for a bereavement, while Charles is sunk in his stunned sense of loss. These are only two examples; each detail of the story unobtrusively serves several purposes at once.

Characters and background are chosen and grouped so as to create four different kinds of structure. This is the story of an individual, her experience shaped by the parallels and contrasts of personal loves, longings, indulgences and frustrations. It is the microcosm of a society; the people who are part of Emma's individual life are chosen to represent from top to bottom the social levels of a French provincial background. And it is what might be called a 'conte philosophique': Flaubert who intensely admired Voltaire and constantly wished to 'jouer avec des idées' isolates and sets in opposition the problems and paradoxes of the basic nature of man and the workings of fate. The same relatively few characters are used for all these three purposes; there is an almost ballet-like precision in the ordering of the outlines. Finally, behind all these run the recurring patterns of a poetic symbolism.

Patterns of Personality

There are three parts to the story of Emma Bovary: the first builds up monotony and frustration through her early life and marriage to Charles; the second a sense of approaching fulfilment with Léon, apparent realisation of all her dreams with Rodolphe, then sudden loss; the third her frenzied efforts at renewal with Léon, her increasing confusion and despair, and her death.

Five men desire her, and Flaubert creates a suggestive structure from the contrasts and likenesses between them. Her husband Charles is the epitome of marvelling devotion, willing to do anything for her, and utterly inadequate to her needs. Charles makes a frame to the story, which begins and ends with him. Begins with him, because the origins, temperament, early life and first marriage of this honest plodder form and explain his utter inability to understand Emma's romanticised desires and despairs, and his almost stupefied delight in her physical loveliness and superior elegance. Ends with him and his child, to show the aftermath of all that Emma's life had caused; to show too how, ironically, it is after her death that he, whose stolidity had so exasperated her when she was alive, becomes affected and extravagant as she herself had been.

Flaubert's construction is very different from the technique of the un-finished 'slice of life'; here, as in *L'Education sentimentale*, the last chapter rounds off the story by rapidly telling what has become of all the main characters.

Charles is the devoted and complacent husband, unable to satisfy his wife either physically or emotionally. Léon has two parts to play; it was only gradually in his plans that Flaubert worked out the idea of using him at separate stages of the novel to show two different kinds of passion. The first is 'platonic' love—two human beings drawn together by what they take to be their superior sensitivity, and 'resisting' their desires; a resistance that leads logically to Emma's seduction by Rodolphe, since she obscurely feels virtue deserves some reward, and is left to the utter emptiness of a feeling that has seeped away into nothing.

Rodolphe is the lover who for a time both fulfils her romantic dreams and satisfies her physical needs. Decisive and skilled in manipulating the sentimental female, he is equally firm and rapid (if faintly regretful) in ridding himself of a clinging encumbrance.

Léon, after his return from Paris, serves the now 'experienced' and disillusioned woman's need both to be consoled and to display to an admiring neophyte the full range of her resources. Whereas Rodolphe had dominated Emma, now it is Emma who dominates, and this in itself brings about her despair and disgust as the veneer of conventional poeticisation peels away to show a young man bored and apprehensive at the possible harvest of his wild oats and sidling rapidly back to bourgeois safety.

Between these apparently contrasting loves, Flaubert weaves patterns and parallels. Each time, Emma hopes for some absolute ecstasy; each time everything falls into a slow decay. An ironical phrase pinpoints the process: 'Elle avait trouvé dans l'adultère toutes les platitudes du mariage.' Charles, Rodolphe and Léon each in turn ceases to be the marvelling possessor of a new delight and becomes the man who takes his regular pleasure as a sheer habit. Rodolphe masters Emma and finds her demands oppressive; Emma masters Léon and is stifled by a sense of emptiness and boredom. Léon and Rodolphe seem opposites, but with each the affair follows the same ineluctable course: resistance, seduction, delight, a growing sense of monotony and disillusion countered by a frantic whipping up of possessiveness, to be met by the weary, instinctive withdrawal of the lover.

Two minor figures add undertones to the theme of the passions.

Guillaumin the notary has been there in the background, but is revealed only at the end, both in his social implications as an ally in the machinations of Lheureux, and in his desire for Emma. The bargain he suggests is too crudely and immediately expressed, his physical appearance and approach as he fondles her knee against the stove too insulting to her delicacy, and she rejects him with the dramatic 'Je suis à plaindre mais pas à vendre'; but as she rushes to Rodolphe, the apparent contrast, Flaubert interjects the grim insinuation of a parallel:

> sans s'apercevoir qu'elle courait s'offrir à ce qui l'avait tantôt si fort exaspérée, ni se douter le moins du monde de cette prostitution.

Guillaumin is the old man attempting to buy physical pleasure. At the opposite extreme is the boy Justin, standing for the calf-love of adolescence, utterly content as long as he can watch and serve his idol, cleaning her shoes and running her errands. He shows a still earlier stage of passion than Léon's 'platonic' love, for he is quite unaware of any possibility of possession. Gradually we see him being disturbed by thoughts of the physical as he watches Félicité ironing Emma's clothes or is caught by Homais reading a book on 'L'amour conjugal'. To the end, Emma remains ironically unconscious of the devotion she has roused in him, just as she ignores the blind adoration of Charles. And other ironies surround this fumbling and frustrated adolescent love. It is Justin, always so anxious to serve Emma, who gives her the key of the poison-cupboard. After her death, while Rodolphe and Léon sleep peacefully, it is Justin, whose worship she never noticed, who is seen sobbing uncontrollably by her grave—seen by the sexton who is certain that the boy is out stealing potatoes. At the end of the book Justin leaves Yonville—in one of Flaubert's plans he ran away to sea, but in the finished novel he becomes a grocer's assistant in Rouen, echoing Léon's abandonment of dream and his retreat into bourgeois existence.

Emma's father and Charles' mother are minor characters, but they appear at key points in the structure of the story. They are chosen to make a contrast: Rouault easy-going, self-indulgent and spendthrift as his daughter will become; Madame Bovary *mère* embittered and frustrated, handing on to her son her devotedness and her love of orderly domestic life while depriving him of all initiative by her obsessive and autocratic care for every detail. She had loved her worthless husband, and lavished on him 'mille servilités qui l'avaient détaché d'elle', just as Emma will weary her lovers by her intensity. But she and Emma show opposite reactions to frustration: where Emma is all impulsive extravagance, Charles' mother has become the epitome of petty convention which deifies economy and suspects any touch of elegance as a sign of perdition. Emma is the neglectful mother; Charles and Léon are the spineless products of narrow, ambitious and implacably devoted maternal care.

At intervals Emma's father provides a background of thoughtless goodwill, Charles' mother of well-meaning exasperation. To the end of the book tiny incidents show the two sides in each of them: Rouault, expansive and easily moved, is desperate at his daughter's death, but removes himself from hurt as quickly as possible, with the kindly and ridiculous consolation that Charles will still have the annual present of a turkey; Charles' mother, possessive to the last, quarrels with her son over Emma's clothes and then because he will not let her have her grandchild to care for.

Charles' father is in his sexual promiscuity a caricature of Rodolphe (and his sensuality appeals to Emma), while his garbled rousseauesque principles for education and bland conviction that no child of his could be a fool offer an echo to Homais. The servant Félicité follows Emma's example, becoming sly, pretentious, neglectful and covetous. In even these minor characters, ironical patterns of parallel and contrast serve both to create sharp individuality and to play variations on central themes.

Structure of Society

The characters who come into Emma's life are selected so as to suggest a social structure. In a small compass we have the range from riches to poverty—from the ball at La Vaubyessard, with the elegant indifference of those used to luxury, ease and intrigue (and in the background, as a relic of the Ancien Régime, the old Duke, to Emma the romantic lover of Marie-Antoinette, but now dribbling and twitching in decrepitude), down to the poor stupefied farm-worker Catherine Leroux, awarded a useless medal for her fifty years of near-slavery, or the hideous blind beggar who haunts the coach on the road from Rouen. In the background stretches the countryside, deliberately chosen as ordinary, average, 'sans caractère', with glimpses of the struggling small-holding families from which Emma and Charles have come, or the shiftless peasant household of the foster-mother Rollet. In the distance is Rouen, the busy city that bemuses Charles when he is a poor student or later goes to the Opera or searches by night for Emma, but to Emma signifies luxury and escape. At the centre Yonville, where the characters who are to affect Emma's life are chosen to give a cross-section of society in a small country-town: chemist, priest, store-keeper, notary, tax-collector, innkeeper, ostler, sexton.

Lheureux is the at first unnoticed but sinister figure in the background, the merchant and money-lender who is gradually forcing his way up through the community; he ruins one of the innkeepers and is in league with the notary. With the cunning of his combined Gascon and Norman background he knows when to flatter and when to exercise blackmail; every manœuvre with Emma is perfectly timed as he changes from the obsequious to the insinuating and then to the brutal. His appearance ('toujours les reins à demi courbés dans la position de quelqu'un qui salue ou qui invite') and the details of his salesman's technique are acutely characterised. His cold skill is bound to triumph: 'Tout lui réussit.'

Two pivotal figures, Homais and Bournisien, are set in opposition: the lay spirit and the clerical spirit, those two vitally opposed forces in the history of nineteenth-century France, here reduced to half-baked cliché-mongers mouthing tenth-hand platitudes. Reduced intellectually, magnified comically and ironically. Homais is the unenlightened apostle of modern enlightenment, the would-be up-to-date man ('il faut marcher avec son siècle') whose ideas are in fact a muddle of incongruous gleanings from Voltaire and Rousseau, mixed with a horde of second-rate out-dated writers, misunderstood and misapplied. Bournisien, who should be the spiritual authority, is better as a help with the hay-making; clumsy, ingratiating, hidebound by routine, he does his best to keep his flock going somehow, adopting a tone of professional colloquialism in trying to bring Hippolyte to Church; attempting to win round Emma in her convalescence by the right kind of bedside chat, 'un petit bavardage câlin qui ne manquait pas d'agrément', as well as indiscriminately ordering for her a set of silly pious tracts. His conscientious futility is contrasted with Homais' unscupulous and menacing success.

These two meet and argue in many scenes as the book goes on, and any subject, from the education of children to the advisability of going to the theatre, will set off between them a barrage of antithetical platitudes. They rise to a climax in their last duet of parrot-lore as they argue by the bedside of the dead Emma:

Lisez Voltaire! lisez l'Encyclopédie!—Lisez les Lettres de quelques juifs portugais! lisez la Raison du Christianisme, par Nicolas, ancien magistrat! (III 9).

Opponents and yet alike, two sides of that mediocre society in which
Emma stifled, they fall asleep by her deathbed, 'après tant de désaccord
se rencontrant enfin dans la même faiblesse humaine', and as they wake,
one claps the other on the shoulder with the phrase, charged in its
context with a bitter irony: 'Nous finirons par nous entendre'! Later,
when Charles has died in poverty and his child has been sent to work in a
mill, Flaubert chooses the most strongly suggestive words to evoke the
unctuous success of the Homais family which 's'étalait, hilare et floris-
sante', and Homais himself reaches social consecration in the final phrase
of the book with its stabbing present tense: 'Il vient de recevoir la croix
d'honneur.'

Homais and Bournisien are the epitome of the idée reçue. Flaubert
planned a Dictionnaire des idées reçues—a compendium of the obligatory
trite ideas of mid-nineteenth-century man and of the mechanical clichés
in which he expresses them. The idée reçue fascinates him not just because
it is representative but because of a particular twist of incongruity. It
may contain idiocies of tautological truism or sheer bland over-simpli-
fication, but the comic clash comes from the fact that the man uttering
it thinks he is expressing something profoundly true, nicely witty,
movingly eloquent, a cut above the ordinary, whereas the expression is
as trite or incongruous as the idea itself. The most sustained examples
come of course in the official speech at the agricultural show (in one plan
Flaubert thought of setting this scene at a prize-giving in a girls' school
and one cannot help wishing that this version too might have been
written). Here all the habitual propagandist encouragements to the man
of toil are glorified into lofty, stereotyped, mixed metaphors, as the
chariot of state struggles in the waves of a stormy sea. One particular
part of the peroration demands expressive reading aloud, to show how
it opens with a weighty reflection, broadens oratorically into a fine
decorative periphrasis, sways with satisfaction across its balanced subsidiary clauses, is suddenly and disastrously unable to maintain its rhetorical momentum, and flounders into bathos on a flat comic monosyllable:

> Qui n'a souvent réfléchi à toute l'importance que l'on retire de ce
> modeste animal, ornement de nos basses-cours, qui fournit à la fois un
> oreiller moelleux pour nos couches, sa chair succulente pour nos
> tables, et . . . des œufs? (II 8).

The agricultural show forms an apex to the book, setting the crisis in
Emma's life against the full festal array of a social system on gala day.

Even as an isolated scene it is a miracle of construction; Flaubert decided to make every one of his Yonville characters figure in it, and set them against the panoply of the national guard, parading firemen, official platform and illuminations. It is typical of provincial unsatisfactoriness that the *préfet* who should have officiated sends a last-minute substitute and that the fireworks have been kept in a cellar and are damp. As the prizes are awarded, for one sudden moment verbose officialdom and stupefied toil stand face to face—and the main characters of the novel remain totally detached from the spectacle.

But the agricultural show is not the only scene of this kind. At intervals in the novel Flaubert has placed typical events that allow him to evoke with high comedy or bitter irony the obligatory social patterns which mould, stifle or stimulate the individual's most important experiences. The village wedding, the christening, the funeral; the ball at the country-house, an evening at the village inn; a visit to the Opera, a conducted tour of Rouen Cathedral: in each of these he can bring alive physical details in all their sharpness or oddity, and set the personal crises of his characters against a background of clamorous cliché. And these type scenes are often suggestively interrelated. In particular, the crisis with Léon in the Cathedral makes a deliberate parallel to the crisis with Rodolphe at the *Comices*. In the earlier scene, Rodolphe persuades Emma of his desire for her against a background of heroico-pastoral historical allusions and of mechanically reiterated announcements of prizes for livestock and vegetables; in the second, Léon's pursuit is systematically interrupted by the Cathedral guide with his automatically repeated patter, as he skims from art and history just that mixture of sentimental anecdote, obsession with factual dimensions, and half-oratorical, half-anecdotal style that should appeal to the public. Both scenes give an almost hallucinatory sense of the insufferable intrusion of the endlessly churning and endlessly repeated preoccupations of the natural, historical or political world on two individuals isolated in their own problems.[1]

They carry other suggestions. First, it is finely fitting that Emma's love-affair with Rodolphe, the sensuous and practical country squire who satisfies her physically, should have its origins in a natural and animal background, and that the crisis with Léon, who always appealed to misty associations with 'higher things', should be set in the Cathedral. It is all

[1] It is worth comparing both scenes with the tour of Fontainebleau by Frédéric and Rosanette in *L'Education Sentimentale*.

the more deliberately ironical that the passion for Rodolphe, with its crude background, should give Emma for a time a kind of frank fulfilment, while the affair with Léon, originating in the would-be platonic and mystical, will lead to frenzied and mechanical artifice.

If the barrel-organ reiteration of social clichés in the background gives an accompaniment of bourgeois *ideés reçues*, the air on the solo instruments is the romantic *idée reçue*. Rodolphe and Emma at the window feel themselves above the world of dull animals or inflated rhetoric, yet it is physical desire which is drawing them together, and Rodolphe's persuasions and Emma's responses are as designedly propagandist or as inflatedly artificial as the speech below. Emma and Léon fly from the conveyor-belt history mouthed by the guide, only to reproduce their own caricatural echo of the passions and luxuries of Diane de Poitiers or Louis de Brézé. Flaubert often uses musical analogies in speaking of the construction of his novel, and certainly to set a trio or a quartet of different clichés working contrapuntally is one of his deepest satisfactions.

Many minor characters give moments of live insight into the social background: the old sewing-woman in Emma's convent, a relic of pre-revolutionary days and an influence on schoolgirl sentimentality and love of small luxuries; the different servants, particularly the orphan Félicité, first eating stolen sugar-lumps over her prayers at night, finally running off with a lover and her mistress's clothes; Hippolyte who is persuaded into his operation out of sexual vanity and above all because 'cela ne lui coûterait rien'; the respectable gossiping village wives, or the crowd that gathers in the hope of a free consultation from the famous doctor. These and many others are sharply characterised in their own right, and also explain and echo the conflicting urges at the centre of the story.

Play of forces

Behind society and individuals, Flaubert constructs patterns of more general implication bearing on the nature of man and of his destiny. The irony of circumstance plays its part. Charles is married off to a supposedly rich widow, but it turns out that her lawyer has absconded with the money. Emma feels that if she could have a son he would be her compensation for the frustrations of woman; it is a daughter who is born. But to show characters as mere victims of events would be to give them a spurious pathos. Flaubert punctures any such idea when Charles at the end of the novel, using a high-sounding phrase for the first time in his life, remarks 'C'est la faute de la fatalité', whereupon we are rapidly brought back to earth by the dry comment: 'Rodolphe, qui avait conduit cette fatalité, le trouva . . . comique.' For other patterns of irony are caused by the conflicting natures of the people involved, as well as by the fact that their desires can never coincide at the right moment. Charles' ugly first wife wearies him by her demands for affection and physical love, just as he will later exasperate Emma with his reiterated caresses and unwavering devotion. At his first wife's death he realises with momentary sorrow that 'elle l'avait aimé, après tout'; Emma on her deathbed will see in his gaze 'une tendresse comme elle n'en avait jamais vu' and wearily recognise 'tu es bon, toi'.

Circumstance and character combine in the logic of what we call fate, as in the phrase from an early version on le père Rouault who made a mess of his farming 'moitié par sa faute, moitié par des hasards'. Rodolphe, who consciously mocks at fatality while writing of it to Emma, yet falls back into asserting he is not to blame for his own nature, 'Moi, je ne peux pas pleurer; ce n'est pas ma faute'. So questions are suggested about the balance of outer and inner pressures and we are left to our own deductions.

Some commentators have imagined that Emma could have been happy in other surroundings or another marriage. Arguing over what she might have been, as over what she ought to have done, is of course different from appreciating an art which so compellingly shows how she is what she is. But Flaubert has answered these speculations above all by the phrase which anatomises her as 'tarissant toute félicité à la vouloir trop grande'.

For through his characters he has constructed a play of forces, showing in extreme form three basic responses made by human beings to the world they live in: those who dream of an impossible absolute, those who unquestioningly accept things as they are, and those who coldly and practically profiteer from whatever circumstances they meet.

Emma pursues 'ideals' of ecstatic passion and total happiness, preconceptions which prevent her ever seeing the world or herself in perspective; she distorts each new experience to fit the mould of her dream, gradually realises that it will not, makes a frenzied and fatal effort to force it back into the mould, then turns desperately to repeating the same sequence in another context, for surely a new place, a new lover, a new feeling will somehow give complete and lasting satisfaction. Léon at first provides a muted echo to this theme, but he is 'd'une nature tempérée', and once his youth is over is destined to end in the camp of the careerists. Emma

C

logically carries her inability to accept the real world to the point of suicide.

Opposite her is Charles, the epitome of unquestioning acceptance, of total and unthinking submission to the nature of things. Incapable of reasoning why, he pursues his daily tasks, uncomplaining in early discomforts, then utterly content with the wife and child fortune has given him, devoted but devoid of imagination or initiative. Catherine Leroux, the poor farm servant seen for a moment at the *Comices*, shows at a still further extreme the same unreflecting service and acceptance. The caricatural echo comes in the tax-official Binet, model of mechanical punctuality and regulated neatness, who sits content, with the peaceful whirr of his lathe for making wooden napkin rings sounding its symbolic refrain. When Emma leans dizzily from the attic window after Rodolphe has abandoned her, this monotonous hum on a blazing and dazzling afternoon is a sensuous part of her hypnotic urge to plunge into nothingness: it is also the ironic contrast to her hankering after the impossible, for Binet has found the mediocre man's solution: unthinking absorption in an unambitious task:

> Binet souriait . . . perdu dans un de ces bonheurs complets, n'appartenant sans doute qu'aux occupations médiocres, qui amusent l'intelligence par des difficultés faciles, et l'assouvissent en une réalisation au-delà de laquelle il n'y a pas à rêver (II 13).

Emma tries wildly to shape reality to what she thinks it should be: Charles with dull humility takes it as it comes. Behind them stand the careerists, the profiteers. These see hard facts, subject them to no ideal, and go firmly about the business of using them to immediate practical advantage. Lheureux has ruined others before Emma, and there comes the symbolic moment at the agricultural show where Mme Lefrançois, who has just recounted one of his financial *coups*, remarks: 'Tenez, le voilà; il salue Madame Bovary.' In the same way Charles is in the power of Homais, that apparently helpful busybody, infinitely pliable to any eventuality, able to make or break the naïve medical officer by journalistic panegyrics or clandestine prescriptions. Lheureux and Homais are the careerists in the world of finance and politics; Rodolphe is the sexual profiteer, an 'esprit positif' who can sum up the crude facts of a situation and manipulate them with skill. These are the hard and practical characters who survive. They have their echo again in a lesser figure, the sexton

Lestiboudois—gardener and odd-job man, making money at the *Comices* by hiring out the Church chairs. He is shown first as profiting from his office by growing potatoes in the graveyard, and at the end, with the same practical and mistaken cynicism as Rodolphe shows in misjudging Emma, he suspects Justin of designs on his crop. Other minor parallels stress the theme of those who are coldly practical: Rodolphe's shedding of a clamorous woman is echoed by Guillaumin's realisation that after all to have made Emma his mistress would scarcely have been worth the complications it would have involved.

Aspiration, acceptance and utilitarianism interplay ironically. We are shown the twists, the oppositions and the paradoxes, and left to reflect.

Network of symbols

Behind people, society, and ideas are other patterns: those of poetic symbolism. A famous example is the echo between the scene where Emma flings her wedding wreath on the fire, the shrivelled petals of the artificial orange-blossom floating off like black butterflies, and the later moment when the torn fragments of her letter rejecting Léon scatter like white butterflies from the window of the cab as she gives in. Or there is the plaster statue of the curé, a piece of provincial prettification in the garden at Tostes, seen at intervals, scaling away under the effect of the weather as Emma's boredom develops, and finally in the move to Yonville smashed to pieces 'sur le pavé de Quincampoix'—at the same time a natural incident in a country removal, a piece of comic onomatopoeia, and a suggestion that Emma's past is being thrown behind her. One small detail, made both precise and suggestive, is taken up in three scenes. As Emma walks through the fields on her wedding day, (I 4) her trailing dress is caught at; Charles stands by, unhelpful and unreflecting, as she picks off the coarse grasses and the barbs of thistles. When she walks with Léon (II 3) honeysuckle and clematis pluck at her parasol; Léon is lost in dreamy delight. In the woods with Rodolphe (II 9), she catches the trailing folds of her riding habit and Rodolphe rejoices in the sensuous suggestions of her gesture.

Chapter 2 of Book I in particular shows clearly how Flaubert can use details to serve several purposes at once. Charles is called out in the night, from his elderly first wife, to deal with the accident to Emma's father; he rides through the dark and arrives at daybreak at the farm. Flaubert is sharply evoking something typical of the life of a country doctor, hauled out of bed, jolting along half-asleep on his horse; typical also of

Charles as an individual, dully trying to recall his scraps of medical know-ledge. Something more general too: the analysis of the state of odd hallucination between sleeping and waking, where the mind loses control of the distinction between past and present and incongruously welds together heterogeneous sensations and memories. But above all, every detail is used to suggest symbolically that Charles is moving from the discomfort and ugliness of the past into a new and rich promise of delight. The rough road, deep ruts, thorny scrub, shivering birds, 'plate campagne', 'surface grise', 'ton morne du ciel'—these are followed by the arrival at the farmyard where every detail conveys prosperity and animation—'une ferme de bonne apparence', 'gros chevaux', 'mangeaient tranquillement', 'rateliers neufs', 'larges fumiers', 'bergerie longue', 'grange haute', 'murs lisses', peacocks which are the 'luxe des basses-cours', and in the background 'le bruit gai d'un troupeau d'oies retentissait'. In the kitchen the details are selected to call up comfort and light —pots boiling, clothes drying in the warmth, while the fire-irons

> tous de proportion colossale, brillaient comme de l'acier poli, tandis que le long des murs s'étendait une abondante batterie de cuisine, où miroitait inégalement la flamme claire du foyer, jointe aux premières lueurs du soleil arrivant par les carreaux.

Behind the objects Charles sees, Flaubert has suggested what is to be the contrast between his past and his future.

Yet as he approaches the farm gate his horse rears in fright—an omen of danger to come. This particular detail has sometimes been considered too contrived; Flaubert has obviously enjoyed parodying a traditional epic device and setting it in the ordinary background of slippery grass and barking farm-dogs.

One minor character has a particularly symbolic part to play: the blind beggar. He comes into the story when Emma has given way to every kind of self-indulgence, and the loathsome disease which eats away his face is like the decay into which her life is falling. But he again serves several purposes. He is used to give a picture of the cruelty of society to the outcast as Hivert hurls crude jokes at him and whips him away from the coach. He suggests how Emma can never face a hideous truth as she shudders away from him or melodramatically flings him her last coin, both to be rid of him and to make the stock gesture of proud despair. He reveals again the stupidity and windy pretentiousness of Homais who urges him to eat good meals, or promises a cure, and the heartless and cowardly change of policy when the cure fails and Homais campaigns in lofty journalistic phrases to have the wretch removed from the public eye. Some critics have felt that there is a touch of romantic melodrama in making him appear when Emma is dying, to haunt her as a spectre of horror. The careful contrivance that prepares this moment may be too obvious, but the suggestions Flaubert draws from it are vital. The beggar conveys the menace of the grotesque behind all human pretensions; there is a fitting irony in making his jingling bawdy song, with its caricature of sensuality and seduction, bite into Emma's last moments. And the details of the song itself are woven into the network of her past. She had already heard it on journeys from Rouen; then it had seemed a gay little fragment full of 'des oiseaux, du soleil et du feuillage'. Now it opens by reducing dreams to their physical origin: 'Souvent la chaleur d'un beau jour | Fait rêver fillette à l'amour'; Emma's life ends with the words 'Et le jupon court s'envola'; while the lines that come between: 'Ma Nanette va s'inclinant | Vers le sillon . . .' recall how her physical attraction first affected Charles through the lovely curve of her body as she bent to pick up the whip he had dropped, or Rodolphe as she stooped to remove a basin from the floor after his servant had been bled. Melodrama would provide one moment of facile and simple shock; it is very different from the deliberate use of poetic stylisation where each detail is used to enrich suggestively the patterns created by people, society and ideas.

3. People[1]

Moi, sous les belles apparences, je cherche les vilains fonds; et je tâche de découvrir, en dessous des superficies ignobles, des mines irrévélées de dévouement et de vertu. (Corr. I 294)

Flaubert wrote in one of his letters:

Ce qui distingue les grands génies, c'est la généralisation dans la création. Ils résument en un type des personnalités éparses et apportent à la conscience du genre humain des personnages nouveaux.

[1] Only certain main characters are discussed in this chapter. For Bournisien, Lheureux and others, see chapters 1, 2 and 4.

A recognisable tendency of the human mind never before crystallised in this way can now be summed up by the word *bovarysme*; and Flaubert, who found Don Quixote just as real and important as Julius Caesar, has made in Homais a figure in its own way as significant as Napoleon.

Création is as vital as *généralisation*. His characters suggest general reflections by coming alive as individuals, with their limitations and mixed motives, the details of the background that has formed them, and their own ways of speaking and thinking: individuals who are not pegs on which the reader may comfortably hang his own feelings, nor puppet-like objects of satire, but provoke a particular kind of critical understanding.

Emma

Flaubert grew up during a period when 'la Recherche de l'Absolu' was glorified. To him, it is precisely the longing for some impossible absolute (a quality deeply ingrained in himself) which may prevent us from coming to terms with the world as it is:

> N'avez-vous pas remarqué que, sans la Conception du Bonheur, l'existence serait plus tolérable. Nous exigeons des choses plus qu'elles ne peuvent donner (*Corr. Supp.* IV 105).

Besides, as the capital letters in this remark suggest, we approach things through a set of inherited preconceptions; the experience of others, or what we read in books, subtly determines what we expect of life. This is the dilemma of any civilised society; La Rochefoucauld had remarked that 'Il y a des gens qui n'auraient jamais été amoureux, s'ils n'avaient jamais entendu parler de l'amour.' Emma Bovary

> cherchait à savoir ce que l'on entendait au juste par ces mots de *félicité*, de *passion*, et d'*ivresse*, qui lui avaient paru si beaux dans les livres.

Absolute concepts and abstract words may distort or mask the individual and relative worth of things as they are; how far are we ever capable of approaching experience directly?

Yet to be without these longings is to risk unreflecting stupidity and complacency: 'Si le sentiment de l'insuffisance humaine venait à périr, nous serions plus bêtes que les oiseaux . . .' In an early version Flaubert wrote an over-rhetorical passage on

> un vague instinct de poésie . . . cet étrange besoin qui tourmente tous les hommes . . . appétit différent selon la capacité des âmes, délicat ou

glouton, enthousiaste ou niais, toujours inassouvi . . . qui fait faire les chefs d'œuvre et les sottises suprêmes (P.L. 296).

The desire for some absolute is both the temptation and the greatness of man; the two possibilities are suggested in Emma.

Her models for the 'ideal' are those of a particular individual and upbringing: they are generally trivial, sentimental and melodramatic. Their cramped and affected formulae both distort and yet suggest with an individual intensity the human urge to make existence echo the great events of history and the stylised beauty of art. At several moments of crisis she remembers not even a book, but a set of painted plates seen once at an inn, depicting the story of La Vallière; Flaubert at the same time plays upon the echoes of a famous historical period, and reduces them to a tiny decorative motif, through which Emma sees herself in trailing robes as a monarch's mistress, image of passion and luxury, or as a mourning nun, image of picturesque repentance. Her reading as a convent school-girl is brilliantly brought alive in details from novels, songs and albums; a concentrated essence of the extravagances of early romanticism and a fine concatenation of the ridiculous, yet with an undertone of odd and haunting appeal. For Emma's very obvious deficiencies are still the outcome of relative and potential qualities; Flaubert spoke of her in his plans as having 'une élégance native, quoique maniérée et fausse souvent'. She is a particularly subtle mixture of delicacy and distortion.

Woman, whether because of something in her nature, or because of inherited traditions and the circumstances imposed on her, may show in exacerbated form the dangers of idealisation. Flaubert's correspondence has several pointed analyses of the muddle-mindedness which may make women unable to see and accept their own nature and needs, or the nature and needs of the necessarily imperfect beings they attach their feelings to:

> Ce que je leur reproche surtout, c'est leur besoin de poétisation . . . Si une femme aime un goujat, c'est un génie méconnu, une âme d'élite, etc., si bien que, par cette disposition naturelle à loucher, elles ne voient pas le vrai quand il se rencontre, ni la beauté là où elle se trouve (*Corr.* II 400).[1]

Above all, they may falsely interpret as emotional or 'spiritual' longings their physical needs: 'Elles ne sont pas franches avec elles-mêmes; elles ne

---

[1] Even here, he sees two sides: "Cette infériorité (qui est, au point de vue de l'amour en soi, une supériorité) est la cause des déceptions . . ."

s'avouent pas leurs sens.' Flaubert's notes and plans express in down-to-earth language what the reader must deduce from indications in the novel: after marriage to Charles 'ses sens ne sont pas encore nés' (in the book we see Charles' expansive pride and her utterly inexpressive demeanour on the day after the wedding); Rodolphe 'lui remue vigoureusement le tempérament'; when she meets Léon in Rouen she is 'mûre des sens cette fois'.

Flaubert, who so sharply punctures the false posturing induced by sentimental conventions, will sometimes convey the intensity and beauty of the experience of the senses with straightforward insight and without immediate irony or deflation. For a brief space the characters feel something directly and do not distort it. That there are other problems involved in the origins and results of that moment, the context makes abundantly clear, but the experience is allowed to be genuine. A post-Lawrentian Emma might have turned to romanticising the physical processes themselves instead of their picturesque and emotional adjuncts; Flaubert's Emma has no models to induce this temptation. At the moment when she finally gives in to Rodolphe, Flaubert creates a purely physiological experience with subtlety and precision. The last sentences open with slow simplicity, expand their phrases with her gradual return to consciousness, culminate in the image which so strongly conveys a sense of complete and rich peace, then trail into the cry in the distance, at the same time suggesting pain, wonder and loveliness, and giving the exact musical equivalent to Emma's last echoing sensations:

> Le silence était partout; quelque chose de doux semblait sortir des arbres; elle sentait son cœur, dont les battements recommençaient, et le sang circuler dans sa chair comme un fleuve de lait. Alors, elle entendit tout au loin, au-delà du bois, sur les autres collines, un cri vague et prolongé, une voix qui se traînait, et elle l'écoutait délicieusement, se mêlant comme une musique aux dernières vibrations de ses nerfs émus (II 9).

This moment rose out of romanticisation and cliché; it will lead to self-congratulation, self-indulgence and disillusion; imaginative understanding is set in critical analysis and so both are strengthened.

It is not that Flaubert is suggesting any over-simplified form of physical pre-conditioning, or making of the recognition of physical needs any absolute solution or value. We have already seen Bournisien satirised for being unable to see beyond this. Of Emma, Flaubert says in his notes: 'L'état sentimental d'Emma l'avait porté aux sens—les sens exaltés la poussent au sentiment.' Like Baudelaire, writing in an age when 'material' and 'spiritual' were too easily accepted as separate and simple terms of insult and praise, he was constantly fascinated, not by their false opposition, but by the idea that physical excess and the desire for some emotional or mystical absolute may be two facets of the same basic urge:

> Je suis convaincu que les appétits matériels les plus furieux se formulent *insciemment* par des élans d'idéalisme, de même que les extravagances charnelles les plus immondes sont engendrées par le désir pur de l'impossible, l'aspiration éthérée de la souveraine joie. Et d'ailleurs je ne sais (et personne ne sait) ce que veulent dire ces deux mots: âme et corps, où l'une finit, où l'autre commence (*Corr.* IV 313),

or, still more pointedly,

> Je ne sais pas ce que veulent dire ces deux substantifs *Matière* et *Esprit* . . . ce ne sont peut-être que deux abstractions de notre intelligence (*Corr.* V 367. See also III 271).

Woman is perhaps (again whether through her nature, conventions or circumstance) particularly liable to make a personal relationship the sole centre of her existence. In Emma Bovary this need or temptation is intensified both by her position and by the kind of person she is. She cannot choose her career; her one hope is to join her life to someone superior who will teach her, admire her, and justify her existence. In the early stages of her marriage, she waits for Charles to show her the answer to the mystery of life, for she feels, however obscurely, a genuine 'besoin d'être développée'—'mais il n'enseignait rien, ne savait rien, ne souhaitait rien'; later she tries again to see herself as the helpmeet of the great doctor, until the fiasco of the club-foot operation. A different woman might have found an outlet in other ways, discovering delight in nature, consolation in religion, the sense of purpose in social charity: Flaubert shows Emma's sporadic incursions into each of these possible solutions, and why they rapidly fail. Here he both relates her to her background and defines her particular character. Brought up on a farm, she is used to the countryside and finds it merely dull; after the brief religiosity of childhood in the convent her 'esprit positif au milieu de ses enthousiasmes' quickly wearies of the intangible, and rejects the demands of doctrine and discipline. This streak of the practical and the careerist is ingrained in her from her peasant background: 'comme la

plupart des gens issus des campagnards, qui gardent à l'âme quelque chose
de la callosité des mains paternelles'. It allows Flaubert, while defining
her, to suggest pointedly another basic problem:

> Il fallait qu'elle pût retirer des choses une sorte de profit personnel; et
> elle rejetait comme inutile tout ce qui ne contribuait pas à la consom-
> mation immédiate de son cœur,—étant de tempérament plus senti-
> mentale qu'artiste (I 6).

To her, personal emotion alone counts, and here, at opposite extremes,
she is like the bourgeois whom she despises. The bourgeois directs all
his efforts towards profiteering in the practical world; Emma is equally
logical and restricted in her emotional profiteering. Both lack the two
qualities that give value to the artist's vision: a capacity to share imaginatively in an experience other than their own ('. . .quoiqu'elle ne
fût guère tendre, ni facilement accessible à l'émotion d'autrui'), and a
disinterested sense of the complexity and wonder of things, enjoyed for
their own sake, not as a means of self-congratulation.

So Emma concentrates with all the more intensity on the search for
the ideal lover. She has no indestructible inner resources which will
remain her own whatever human beings do to her: her drawing or
piano-playing mean nothing to her if there is no lover to share or admire, and she abandons them with a weary 'à quoi bon'. Through her
is seen in particular form the general problem of the woman to whom
no detail of living has value or meaning unless all life can be centred
on one satisfactory human being. In Emma this involves at the same
time the genuine urge to communicate indefinable but intense possibilities—

> Si Charles l'avait voulu, cependant, s'il s'en fût douté, si son regard,
> une seule fois, fût venue à la rencontre de sa pensée, il lui semblait
> qu'une abondance subite se serait détachée de son cœur . . .

—and the need to find in a lover an instrument to self-esteem.

This search is set in a woman who is 'incapable de croire à tout ce
qui ne se manifestait pas par des formes convenues'. The attempt to live
up to a stereotyped model has three results. First the artificial whipping
up of feeling: 'd'après des théories qu'elle croyait bonnes, elle voulut
se donner de l'amour.' Then, an inability to appreciate anything that
does not fit the model: Emma tries the comically inapposite stimulus of
reciting passionate poetry to Charles by moonlight when he is merely
thankful to get off his horse and have a good meal; as he does not react

romantically she overlooks his intense if inarticulate feeling, and concludes that this cannot be Love; or her passion for Léon develops slowly, so for long she does not recognise it, since Love must start as a *coup de foudre*. Finally there is the complacent contemplation of emotion once it has been forced to fit the conventional mould.

In his correspondence Flaubert expressed his hatred of those who unctuously and dramatically display with a flourish feelings which they falsify by pretentious parade:

> ceux qui vous parlent de leurs amours envolés, . . . baisent des médailles, pleurent à la lune, délirent de tendresse en voyant des enfants, prennent un air pensif devant l'Océan . . . qui font le saut de tremplin sur leur propre cœur (*Corr.* II 462).

Throughout the novel, Emma both literally and metaphorically watches with loving admiration her own attitudes seen in a mirror: the real mirror before which she sits gazing at herself after being seduced by Rodolphe, and the mirror of inherited preconceptions, as she realises with delight that she now fits into a category and a tradition:

> J'ai un amant! un amant! Alors elle se rappela les héroïnes des livres qu'elle avait lus, et la légion lyrique ces femmes adultères se mit à chanter dans sa mémoire avec des voix de sœurs (II 9).

This self-consciousness is all the more insidious when it is part of apparent virtue. Emma makes repeated attempts to be a 'good wife and mother', but unexceptionable attitudes are undermined by exaggeration, by the sheer self-satisfaction in her way of expressing them, and by the grimly simple categories they create: 'Une bonne mère de famille ne s'inquiète pas de sa toilette . . . n'ai-je pas ma maison à tenir, mon mari à soigner, mille choses enfin, bien des devoirs . . .' Or Flaubert makes the direct comment, with the added insinuation of the verb *croyait*:

> Puis l'orgueil, la joie de se dire: 'Je suis vertueuse', et de se regarder dans la glace en prenant des poses résignées, la consolait un peu du sacrifice qu'elle croyait faire (II 5).

Sometimes she creates the mirror-image of the ideal mother, exaggerated vocabulary or gesture indicating her self-adulation:

> elle déclarait adorer les enfants, c'était sa consolation, sa joie, sa folie, et elle accompagnait ses caresses d'expansions lyriques;

more usually she rejects the child precisely because it spoils the stereotyped picture of ideal maternity: it is sick over her collar or looks ugly under tear-stains and sticking-plaster.[1]

Through Emma, Flaubert has analysed the problems of forced emotion, curiosity and complacency in any love-affair, and those of self-satisfaction and ostentation in what might be taken for granted as virtue. Emma herself shows to a particular degree self-consciousness without self-knowledge; at intervals it is stressed that she has no sense of guilt. This both provokes critical judgment and yet gives to her character a kind of frank and logical intensity in the pursuit of her needs, suggested in the recurring and deliberately ambiguous use of the word 'candeur' to describe her.

The more intensely she strives, the more her different experiences follow the same inevitable sequence: longing, apparent achievement, then the sudden or slow sense of emptiness, monotony, disintegration, to be followed by the artificial whipping up of a new illusion. Is this because she meets only unsatisfactory people and circumstances, or because of her own limitations, or because ecstasy by its very nature cannot last? All three may be suggested, and contrasting reflections provoked.

From the beginning in the convent, her first passion for religion or her grief at her mother's death shows the adolescent attempt to achieve a picturesque and emotional ideal, followed by weariness and the refusal to recognise plain facts:

> Emma fut intérieurement satisfaite de se sentir arrivée du premier coup à ce rare idéal des existences pâles, où ne parviennent jamais les cœurs médiocres . . . Elle s'en ennuya, n'en voulut point convenir, continua par habitude, ensuite par vanité . . . (I 6).

Much later, during her nervous collapse after Rodolphe has left her, she turns again to religion (II 14). Her physical illness gives an ecstatic sensuous hallucination; we see at the same time the obligatory appurtenances of angels, harps and palms, the genuine weary longing to lose the pride and the strivings of the individual, the relic of self-consciousness in 'savourant le plaisir d'être faible', and above all the hope of a delight that will everlastingly increase (the long adverb coming as a deliberate climax):

[1] The child Berthe, seen so little because she matters so little to Emma, is brought clearly alive in her deprivation: clinging, plaintive, inconsequent, tearful, frightened, unable to concentrate.

un autre amour au-dessus de tous les autres amours, sans intermittence ni fin, et qui s'accroîtrait éternellement.

But once this vision has disappeared, her feelings refuse to remain at the same high pitch: 'elle *s'efforçait* d'en ressaisir la sensation'. Bournisien's clumsy and arrogant tracts bore her; her own impulsive and undiscriminating desires are shown in all their incongruity in the sentence:

Elle voulut devenir une sainte . . . elle souhaitait avoir dans sa chambre, au chevet de sa couche, un reliquaire enchâssé d'émeraudes.

Her exaggerated intensity disquiets the poor curé as it will frighten her lovers and finally her confused effort to stimulate feeling falls back into weariness and disillusion:

Quand elle se mettait à genoux sur son prie-Dieu gothique, elle adressait au Seigneur les mêmes paroles de suavité qu'elle murmurait jadis à son amant. . . . C'était pour faire venir la croyance; mais aucune délectation ne descendait des cieux; et elle se relevait, les membres fatigués, avec le sentiment vague d'une immense duperie.

(Her desires are conveyed by words which both in sound and meaning suggest a caressing, half-sensuous, half-abstract delight: *suavité*, *délectation*, and the contrast is put not in the plain form of 'she felt she had been deceived', but tails out in the vast empty abstraction: 'le sentiment vague d'une immense duperie'.)

Her effort at humanitarianism is as exaggerated, impulsive and undiscriminating: for a short time she obsessively knits vests for orphans instead of getting on with the housework, invites tramps into the kitchen, and sends the servant to enjoy herself with her lover.

Art provokes the same sequence of reactions. In the Opera she sees only what is like or unlike her own feelings. Here there occurs the brilliantly-worded sentence on that ridiculous and all too understandable dream of the absolute which with its own incongruous logic imagines every possible need solved at once and perfection indefinitely prolonged:

Ah! si . . . elle avait pu placer sa vie sur quelque grand cœur solide, alors la vertu, la tendresse, les voluptés et le devoir se confondant, jamais elle ne serait descendue d'une félicité si haute (II 15).

The centre of her life is the search for a hero, and we can best see her individual nature and the wider suggestions behind it by comparing the similar origins, climaxes and failures of her successive love-affairs.

The origins of her ill-assorted marriage are rapidly told; we have a clear picture of the 'jeune fille' fresh from the convent, isolated and bored in the country, thinking herself, as youth so often does, highly experienced and loftily disillusioned, responding to the physical and emotional challenge of the first possible suitor, curious to see what the experience of marriage will mean. A conversation on her health, her music, her school prizes, her mother's grave, and the difficulty of managing servants shows her appealing in turn for sympathy and admiration. Rapidly she comes to believe 'qu'elle possédait enfin cette passion merveilleuse.'

In the 'platonic' love-affair with Léon, we have seen how the two are drawn together by unrecognised physical attraction and romantic dissatisfactions and longings, and how Emma does not at first realise her feelings. When she does, it is as much because of the sheer contrast with the crude and irritating Charles, stumping clumsily in the fields on a cold Sunday afternoon, as because of any of Léon's own qualities; the theme of how each lover will profit from the deficiencies of the husband, brought alive in the petty detail of everyday life, will constantly recur. Emma's obsession with Léon grows, and Flaubert analyses the basic feelings that may be part of any experience of falling in love: desire to know his every movement, every detail of his surroundings, jealousy of those who come near him, the giving of the kind of present that will be a constant reminder, the necessity to hide love but longing for some accident that might reveal it—all this with a deliberate undertone of the comic when it is the fat, kindly Madame Homais, 'la meilleure épouse de la Normandie, douce comme un mouton' who is envied for sleeping beneath the same roof.

Léon, in contrast to Charles, seemed delicate and 'poetic'; Rodolphe is another contrast: masterful and worldly. In his opening discussions with Emma the most basic arguments of the persuasive lover are both represented and caricatured—the loneliness beneath the surface, the need for someone who could share and inspire a worth-while life, the incidental appeal to the attraction of an experienced lover, mingled with arguments on the higher virtue which disdains convention, the need to develop one's sensibilities, passion as the source of what is finest in man, the value of total sacrifice. Deliberately Flaubert moves between the obvious clichés of the romantic virtuoso in a mood for seduction (moonlight, graveyards, madonnas, angels and decrees of fate) and the bare and clear words that anyone might have used: 'J'ai besoin de vous . . .' The reader is driven to reflect on the arguments and expression of feeling in general, and if we are set at a critical distance from the scheming seducer and the bemused woman, we are made to see with intensity the inner effect on Emma as for the first time all her needs seem to be realised.

> C'était la première fois qu' Emma s'entendait dire ces choses ; et son orgueil . . . s'étirait mollement et tout entier à la chaleur de ce langage.

The origins of the second stage with Léon form one of the richest scenes of the book (III 1). Emma now believes that she is too adult and experienced to be deluded by stock romanticism, and when Léon pretends that he has found her hotel by instinct or fate she gives a smile, making him hastily change his tactics. This time it is Emma who leads the conversation, as they take up the eternal litany of lamentation of frustrated lovers. Again the central feelings are those that might seriously be felt by any two people who loved, separated, and met again, given intense irony by the mixed motives and the expression in this particular scene. It opens with the theme of duty and loneliness, leads on to the uselessness of a wasted life, which one would so gladly have devoted to some practical sacrifice, and ends with the dream of what might have been. The comic exaggeration in Léon's picture of Emma as a Muse crowned with forget-me-nots or the irony of Emma's vision of herself as a devoted nurse, capped by Léon's idea of himself as a doctor (the profession of her despised husband; Emma hastily changes the subject) is mingled with their memories of tiny details in their past, and the long silence when they can find no way of expressing what they feel.

Neither has told the full truth; a bare, balanced sentence points out that 'Elle ne confessa point sa passion pour un autre; il ne dit pas qu'il l'avait oubliée.' From the present they unconsciously weave a false past:

> car c'est ainsi qu'ils auraient voulu avoir été, l'un et l'autre se faisant un idéal sur lequel ils ajustaient à présent leur vie passée.

The mere use of words gradually creates belief (a theme other penetrating novelists have explored, Marivaux and Constant among them), and we are left with the suggestive general reflection:

> D'ailleurs, la parole est un laminoir qui allonge toujours les sentiments.

Between the origins and the fulfilment of passion may come the stage of resistance. In the first episode with Léon it has many mixed motives The mere discovery of love may in itself be so satisfying that there is a momentary pause with no urge to go further (a theme to which Stendhal, using it differently, often gives a particular gaiety and bite). Then the attitude of the 'bonne mère de famille', warming her husband's slippers, kissing him demonstratively and enthusing over the child, is made possible because of the intimate delight of knowing that Léon desires her (and throughout the book will recur ironical moments when Emma charms her husband because she is happy with her lover): it serves also as a provocation to Léon. There is besides the pleasure of being able to say 'Comme j'ai été sage.' But if Emma and Léon go no further at this stage, it is chiefly because neither dares to take a decisive step; they sit face to face, each desperately wondering what lies behind the restraint of the other.

In keeping with the more intense and positive feeling between Emma and Rodolphe, the scene where her resistance is overcome (II 9) brings out the bare instinctive conflict of elemental reactions: desire and fear. The background and Emma's feelings are caught together in a sense of hesitant expectancy and uncertain menace. Against the breadth of sky, the warm stillness and ripe autumn colours, among the tangled bracken and by the stagnant pond, with rustling in the undergrowth and the timid hopping of frogs in the pool, Flaubert sets her gestures of longing and of retreat. One adverb, significantly placed, suggests what the end is bound to be: 'Elle tâchait de se dégager mollement.' Rodolphe makes full use of his experienced technique, but here Emma's own words are brief and breathless, leaving her no time for phraseology or pose: 'Vous me faites peur! Vous me faites mal! Partons.'

When she meets Léon again in Rouen her effort to resist is already undermined by past memories, the need to be consoled for hurt pride and loss, and his apparent contrast with Rodolphe. Realising with sudden terror that Léon's timidity is an even more dangerous attraction than was Rodolphe's decisiveness she writes her letter of renunciation: the very fact that it is 'interminable' shows her hesitation. In the Cathedral she looks to religion for some miraculous outside force which will save her, but her efforts to lose herself in the sense-impressions of scents, splendours and silence only increase the tension. Finally she gives in to danger under the impulse of snobbery: she enters the cab with Léon because 'Cela se fait à Paris', just as she had agreed to go riding with Rodolphe because of the fashionable riding-habit:'L'amazone la décida'.

The illusion of fulfilment has practically no place in her marriage except when she at first enjoys displaying her gifts as an elegant housewife. With Léon in the early stages there is delicately conveyed the gradual growth of an unrecognised attraction, sometimes presented critically, sometimes allowed a momentary loveliness, particularly as they walk back along the river bank from the visit to the nurse, surrounded by summer sights and sounds, lost in undefined present pleasure and vague anticipation:

> surpris d'étonnement à cette suavité nouvelle, ils ne songeaient pas à s'en raconter la sensation ou en découvrir la cause (II 3).

With Rodolphe for a time Emma's senses are satisfied, and she seems to have found the eloquent and masterful lover her dream required. Her sense of savouring a triumphant vengeance on life, and her complete lack of any feeling of guilt towards Charles may act as distancing devices, but Flaubert has analysed something general about what he calls in his notes the 'orgueil de l'initiation', and has created in detail the delight and gaiety of her morning visits to Rodolphe as, while he is still asleep, she appears, fresh with the scents of the country, blinking in the first sunlight, her hair wet with the dew and her feet muddy from the slippery riverside path.

The first days with Léon in Rouen carry many suggestions (III 5). The boat setting out in the evening through the everyday sights and sounds of Rouen harbour is a deliberate parody of the honeymoon gondola of tradition, and Emma singing Lamartine's *Le Lac* with eyes upturned to heaven adds the final touch of the inappropriate. Then there is the dry bite in the comment on those who appreciate the beauty of nature only when it is enhanced by irrelevant passions:

> Ce n'était pas la première fois qu'ils apercevaient des arbres, du ciel bleu, du gazon, qu'ils entendaient l'eau couler et la brise soufflant dans le feuillage; mais ils n'avaient sans doute jamais admiré tout cela, comme si la nature n'existait pas auparavant, ou qu'elle n'eût commencé à être belle que depuis l'assouvissance de leurs désirs.

Yet meantime in the background is the subtle loveliness of the real world which the romantic dream neglects: the echo of the caulking hammer on the hull of ships, the spiral of smoke from the hot tar, the patterns made by mooring-ropes, and their sound as they brush aslant against the boats, the shifting patches of oil floating on the water, bronze-coloured in the last rays of the sun.

This is the substitute passion of an 'experienced' and older woman, who finds pleasure in initiating Léon as Rodolphe had initiated her. It is intensified by being both a sudden rebirth after loss and despair, and a return

D

across the years to a shared past. But its intensity has the tone of the hyper-civilised and artificial. The love-affair with Rodolphe had the crude or fresh countryside as a setting; that with Léon is evoked mainly in the closed hotel bedroom, with as a background the city of Rouen and the sensations and associations of luxury it holds for Emma:

> On sentait l'absinthe, le cigare et les huîtres . . . Quelque chose de vertigineux se dégageait pour elle de ces existences amassées, et son cœur s'en gonflait abondamment . . . La vieille cité normande s'étalait à ses yeux comme une capitale démesurée, comme une Babylone où elle entrait (III 5).

Disillusion follows its inevitable but very varied course. For the period of early frustration with Charles, Flaubert, who wrote in his correspondence that love is less a matter of inflated sentiment than of not getting on each other's nerves in the smallest things,[1] conveys the insupportable galling exasperation of trivial but grating detail in day-to-day life. Emma is faced with Charles' noisy swallowing of soup, excavating of his teeth with his tongue after meals, clumsy clothes, deadly dull conversation, muddy boots and snoring at night. The ball at La Vaubyessard seems to promise a new outlet, and the Vicomte who danced with her becomes a dream-figure in contrast with the clumsy Charles. But a whole year goes by and there is no new invitation. Flaubert builds up through the obsessive rhythm and detail of his sentences the crushing and claustrophobic monotony of her empty days:

> Tous les jours, à la même heure . . . Soir et matin . . . De temps à autre . . . Elle le voyait toujours là . . . Dans l'après-midi . . .,

ending with the barrel-organ and its mechanical dancing figures, symbol at the same time of the automatism of her daily life and of the longing for exotic places called up by the tunes. Gradually the alternation of weary negligence and wild impulse works up to her first nervous collapse.

When she discovers that Léon desires her, she sits in solitude delighting in her mental image of him. The reality is different. One brief sentence is constructed so as to rise in anticipation, interpose his sudden appearance, fall into blank anti-climax, and trail away in prolonged emptiness:

> Emma palpitait au bruit de ses pas: puis, en sa presence, l'émotion tombait, et il ne lui restait ensuite qu'un immense étonnement qui se finissait en tristesse (II 5).

[1] *Corr.* II 12, 41, 289.

Nothing happens and eventually Léon leaves for Paris. Regret, like anticipation, transforms the reality: she makes Léon in memory 'plus grand, plus beau, plus suave, plus vague', and when even memory begins to be blotted out by absence and habit, she whips up her exasperation with Charles into imagined love for the lost Léon.

If here her disillusion came from a passion which was frustrated, fulfilment brings in the end no happier result and works with a bitter inner logic. Her eager delight begins to harass Rodolphe, who covers exasperation by fine phrases about fear of compromising her. She who had wanted a masterful lover begins to resent the logical consequences: his power and her own dependence. Once the first novelty is over, Rodolphe comes to take for granted an ironically regular relationship which drags on its way till suddenly a homely affectionate letter from her father faces Emma with the contrast between her past dreams and the indefinable but terrifying insufficiency of the present. She quarrels with Rodolphe, returns to Charles (the husband this time profiting from the contrast with the failings of the lover) and tries to see herself as the devoted wife until the catastrophe of the bungled operation.

In the second stage with Rodolphe, renewed passion is whipped up by disgust at Charles' failure, and by increasing artifice. She gives way to every impulse, lavishes presents on Rodolphe, submits to his calculated experiments in eroticism, and more and more stifles him with her clamorous possessiveness. Once again it is a petty event which precipitates crisis: a quarrel with her mother-in-law over how to treat the servants makes her beg Rodolphe to take her away for good.

Deliberately Flaubert stresses that it is at this particular stage that Emma is at the height of her beauty and charm; he leaves to the reader the moral and aesthetic implications of his general comment:

Elle avait cette indéfinissable beauté qui résulte de la joie, de l'enthousiasme, du succès, et qui n'est que l'harmonie du tempérament avec les circonstances . . . Elle s'épanouissait enfin dans la plénitude de sa nature (II 12).

The image in which he conveys this may well remind us of the title and many of the poems of the *Fleurs du Mal*:

Ses convoitises, ses chagrins, l'expérience du plaisir et ses illusions toujours jeunes, comme font aux fleurs le fumier, la pluie, les vents et le soleil, l'avaient par gradation développée . . .

'Ses illusions toujours jeunes': She has once again forced a dream of escape, and anticipation, like memory, gives the delight which her real experience can never prolong.

In the second stage with Léon, her disillusion is already implicit in the fear left from the past: 'Ah! tu me quitteras, toi . . . tu seras comme les autres'—and fear intensifies her possessiveness. Her experienced sensuality, which had first delighted Léon, eventually makes him suspicious or weary. Emma had seen in him a contrast to Rodolphe, an attractively timid and poetic lover: again ironical logic follows its course as she discovers his parsimony and spinelessness. The comic scene of Homais' visit to Rouen brings this to a head; Emma in a fury sees Léon as 'faible, banal, mou, avare et pusillanime', then shifts, as those who are afraid of destroying their love or their illusions always will, to making excuses for him; but the damage is done, for

> le dénigrement de ceux que nous aimons toujours nous en détache quelque peu.

The effort to rouse flagging passion takes two forms: the romantic embroidery in letters full of poetry, flowers and moonlight, 'ressources naïves d'une passion affaiblie, qui essayait de s'aviver à tous les secours extérieurs', and the frantic sensuality which produces only a mechanically renewed sequence of anticipation, flat emptiness and further pursuit:

> Elle se promettait continuellement, pour son prochain voyage, une félicité profonde; puis elle s'avouait ne rien sentir d'extraordinaire.

Just as she had first attracted then wearied Rodolphe by her morning visits, so her appearances at Léon's office, originally charming and flattering, become a threat. Léon longs to escape from her domination, but feels a drugged inertia, experiencing the same mixture of fear, fury and obsession as Emma had felt for Rodolphe.

Again Emma fully realises what is happening only when the past breaks in on the present: this time as she sits to rest outside the convent where she spent her childhood, and suddenly sees Léon on the same level of distant unreality as all the other illusions that have failed. Yet, as in the last stages of many liaisons, neither can break the ties that hold them. Emma goes on writing 'en vertu de cette idée qu'une femme doit toujours écrire à son amant', and makes of her letters a last desperate dream addressed to the ideal lover she would have wished him to be, indulging in still another imaginative paroxysm, followed by a dull void.

The last moments of each love-affair sum up its particular atmosphere and carry wide suggestions. As Léon leaves for Paris at the end of the 'platonic' stage (II 6), Flaubert creates a scene in which the reader is made aware of an almost unbearably tense emotion unable to find more than banal words or silent gestures. Léon tries to grasp and absorb into himself every detail of her surroundings in one last look 'comme pour pénétrer tout, emporter tout', and as he touches her hand 'la substance même de tout son être lui semblait descendre dans cette paume humide'. Yet all they can manage to express is the trivial daily interchange, with its undertone of protection and reassurance, and its flat end: 'Il va pleuvoir' —'J'ai un manteau'—'Ah!'—and so he leaves.

The last evening with Rodolphe (II 12) is evoked in a passage outstanding for its sensuous loveliness and for the combined irony and tenderness it suggests. In full consciousness of the bitter implications, we are allowed a pause to share their sensations and feelings—Emma turning towards the future, yet with a haunting apprehension of insufficiency; Rodolphe knowing that he will leave her, but caught by a last sense of charm and regret; both half-hypnotised by the warmth of the night air and the play of scents, shadows and sounds. All the details of the background echo the personal experience of a luxuriant beauty and a hidden threat: the moonlight twists like the gleaming scales of a serpent as it falls on the river that flows inevitably away; in the grass there is the rustle of prowling weasel or hedgehog, and the soft sound of a ripe peach falling to the ground. As they sit in silence

La tendresse des anciens jours leur revenait au cœur, abondante et silencieuse comme la rivière qui coulait . . .

The spell is broken by speech; seizing the opportunity of Emma's sudden apprehension, Rodolphe tries to persuade her not to leave with him. Her reply, epitomising the dream of absolute passion, ironically brings to a concentrated climax that frenzy of cloying possessiveness which makes him break with her:

A mesure que nous vivrons ensemble, ce sera comme *une étreinte chaque jour plus serrée, plus complète* . . . Nous serons *seuls, tout à nous,* éternellement.

In the final scene with Léon (III 7), both characters have already worn out all sensuality or emotion; practical need provokes a dry, bare discussion, punctuated by Emma's demands and taunts.

There is a last return to Rodolphe, and a last break (III 8). As always, Emma misinterprets her own motives and is blandly unaware that initially she has gone back to sell herself. Yet, as she runs through the countryside, something else comes to the fore:

> Elle se retrouvait dans les sensations de sa première tendresse, et son pauvre cœur comprimé s'y dilatait amoureusement.

When it seems that Rodolphe is ready to renew their love, her words show the desperate submission of the woman who will accept any condition (no matter about his other mistresses—'Tu es un homme, toi') and be deliberately gay to please him ('Tiens, je ris'). Her tears, her beauty and her intensity win him over; as always, she thinks of money as the most minor of matters. When he refuses, in her last burst of disillusion we see both the genuine suffering of the rejected woman and her confusion about herself. She flings him among all who have failed her, looks back with anguish to question why he seduced her—was she no more than a challenge to male pride?—bitterly and with unconscious irony reproaches him with the idea that 'sans toi j'aurais pu vivre heureuse', and scornfully contrasts her own spendthrift intensity of passion with his practical love of ease and comfort. When she leaves, as always with Emma, emotion has blotted out everything else:

> Elle ne se rappelait point la cause de son horrible état, c'est-à-dire la question d'argent. Elle ne souffrait que de son amour.

Passion and pride, neither clear-sighted about itself, remain her conscious motives to the end. She has loftily rejected Guillaumin; she cannot appeal to Charles, for her vanity cannot bear the thought that he, so inferior, will forgive her. She turns to suicide as the last stereotype of self-congratulation: 'dans un transport d'héroïsme qui la rendait presque joyeuse . . . presque dans la sérénité d'un devoir accompli.' When dying, she imagines she has renounced her past, realises the devotion of Charles and asks to see her child; but the search for an all-enveloping passion is still ineradicable as she imprints on the crucifix 'le plus grand baiser d'amour qu'elle eût jamais donné', while her last living act is to ask in a clear voice for her mirror and to weep hopelessly over what she sees there.

Behind Emma's experiences, Flaubert makes other suggestions about human nature and human behaviour. Some critics have thought that her financial extravagance is introduced to make her an individual (or because of particular models Flaubert is supposed to have used), and that it is not a typical or necessary consequence of her other passions. But Flaubert has shown how once the senses are roused, both frustration and indulgence may intensify the urge to spend lavishly—a consolation when passion is deprived, a celebration when it is fulfilled. The details are made part of the individual Emma:[1] she inherits a love of comfort from her easy-going father, and takes from her romantic models the idea that a unique and intense passion must be set in surroundings of picturesque luxury. But the sentimental or frivolous signs—the seal engraved 'amor nel cor', the elegant riding whip or the bottles of champagne—stand for the mixed motives that may lie in differing proportions behind any desire to shower gifts on a lover—generosity, convention, semi-bribery and impulsive self-indulgence. Flaubert is interested too in a physiological analysis of the means used by a particular temperament to stimulate or soothe the nervous system, as in the details of Emma's use of scents or sudden craving for certain kinds of food and drink.

The vagaries of the human memory are another theme on which conflicting reflections are suggested. The mind may conveniently transfigure or even blot out whole stretches of the past—as when Emma and Léon talk in Rouen. And when it most desires to preserve a memory, it may find this most impossible—as with Emma after Léon first leaves, or more bitterly with Charles after Emma's death:

> Une chose étrange, c'est que Bovary, tout en pensant à Emma continuellement, l'oubliait; et il se désespérait à sentir cette image lui échapper de la mémoire au milieu des efforts qu'il faisait pour la retenir.

But at the opposite extreme, the mind may unconsciously preserve past desires and experiences in a confused amalgam; Emma beside Rodolphe at the *Comices* is for a moment seized by vertiginous memories of the Vicomte and Léon, and later, sitting by the convent wall, fuses childhood, the ball, Rodolphe and Léon in one terrible moment of crumbling disillusion. Often it is a sudden sense-impression, as later with Proust,

[1] Even in the scene towards the end where she has gone in desperation to beg for money from Guillaumin, she pauses to notice 'Voilà une salle-à-manger comme il m'en faudrait une.'

that calls up these linked memories. Not, as in Proust, with a sense of triumph over time, but rather as conveying the undiscriminating equality in the necropolis of the human heart.

Flaubert deliberately plays variations on generally accepted ideas about the contrast between the nature of man and the nature of woman. The refrain 'Tu es un homme, toi', 'Car enfin vous n'êtes pas une femme, vous', and that of the inability of each sex to understand the other's problems, runs through his characters' conversations. Rodolphe and Emma in their central scene in the woods play the part of the 'type' male and female: the woman lost in the prolonged repercussions of her physical experience, the man rapidly satisfied ('Rodolphe, le cigare aux dents . . .'). Emotionally too the woman has made of love her one centre, while in both Rodolphe and Léon there is brought alive their instinctive and comprehensible retraction before the stifling possessiveness of the female, their sheer fear of being loved or tied too much.

Writing of Rodolphe who, having deserted Emma with a letter which speaks of meeting again in quiet friendship, then took care to keep out of her way, Flaubert used the phrase 'cette lâcheté qui caractérise le sexe fort'. For the concept of 'le sexe fort' is an *idée reçue*, and he will delight in showing what unexpected factors may contradict conventional ideas about male or female. Baudelaire, himself fascinated by this problem, perhaps over-stressed the 'masculine' qualities in Emma, but Flaubert has certainly deliberately opposed her active and decisive nature to that of the timorous and malleable Léon, and set her neglect of her household and child in contrast to Charles' ingrained love of domesticity and tender detailed care for Berthe—qualities expected rather of the wife and mother. There is both an undertone of deliberate parody and a sense of human complexity in this ironical reversal of roles.

Léon (see also pp. 15–21, 31–33, 46–56, 69, 71, 77)

Léon, like Emma, dreams the stereotyped dream. To sunsets and the Alps he adds visions of Student Life in Paris, a hotch-potch of the bohemian clichés of the day (masked balls, grisettes, a room decorated by fencing foils, a skull and a guitar). When he possesses Emma, he sees in her the compendium of all that a young man of the time aspires to conquer:

n'était-ce pas *une femme du monde*, et une femme mariée! une vraie maîtresse enfin? Elle était l'amoureuse de tous les romans, l'héroïne de tous les drames, le vague *elle* de tous les volumes de vers . . .

l'odalisque au bain . . . le corsage long des châtelaines féodales . . . la femme pâle de Barcelone . . . l'Ange (III 5).

The stereotype today would be different; the exultation of grasping at what is traditionally desirable remains. Léon thinks himself a superior spirit, but represents exactly that degree of timid and moderate experimentation with the arts and the passions which conventional society will pride itself on broad-mindedly allowing to a young man before he settles down. The inhabitants of Yonville find he has 'des manières *comme il faut*'. He has no political convictions, and as for the artistic gifts on which he prides himself, Flaubert in one dry sentence suggests their extent and importance: 'il possédait des talents, il peignait à l'aquarelle, savait lire la clef de sol, et s'occupait volontiers de littérature après son dîner, quand il ne jouait pas aux cartes.' In Paris he was 'le plus convenable des étudiants'. In the end, manipulated by his mother and by the head of his office, he moves back into bourgeois careerist convention, and marries a Mlle Léocadie Lebœuf—Léocadie, recalling one of the romantic names Emma had thought of for her child; Lebœuf and her home in Bondeville insinuating stolid practicality. Flaubert adds the general reflection:

car tout bourgeois, dans l'échauffement de sa jeunesse, ne fût-ce qu'un jour, une minute, s'est cru capable d'immenses passions, de hautes entreprises . . . Chaque notaire porte en soi les débris d'un poète (III 6).

Manipulated by his mother: even in the early stages when he is weary of Yonville and plans to leave for Paris Léon puts off deciding anything until she steps in and organises. He is attracted by Emma's maternal poses when he sees her with her child; in their later passion she calls him 'Enfant'. The love for the older woman as a mother-figure is both seriously characterised and associated critically with a hesitant and indecisive temperament. The scene of Homais' visit to Rouen shows Léon trailing feebly in the wake of the jovial chemist, and Flaubert reflects on the odd half-hypnotised spinelessness that lets us give way to this kind of drift 'par lâcheté, par bêtise, par cet inqualifiable sentiment qui nous entraîne aux actions les plus antipathiques'.

Flaubert commented in his correspondence (I 417) on those who think that because a feeling is moderate, tepid or sporadic it is therefore uninteresting or almost non-existent. The 'sentiments tièdes' are in their own way as authentic as the stronger passions and demand more subtle rendering. Léon, a predecessor of Frédéric in *L'Education sentimentale*, is indecisive and lacks persistence, but his early feeling for Emma ('timide et profond') is brought alive in their walks together and in his intense wordless longing as they part.[1]

He is an echo to Charles in his malleability and lack of enterprise, a contrast in his semi-sophistication and his lack of devoted affection. In the early relationship between the two, Flaubert has suggested a situation that again he will more fully analyse in *L'Education sentimentale*. Instead of seizing the opportunity to find Emma alone, Léon willingly spends his time with her husband, and in their farewell scene he asks to see her child. Here Flaubert is able at the same time to reverse the convention by which two men who love the same woman are jealous rivals, and to suggest something deeply rooted in human psychology: first the urge to know and share everything that belongs to the life of the loved person ('Son mari n'était-ce pas quelque chose d'elle?'), then, still more important, the obscure need of the outsider not so much to love and conquer an individual woman as to make himself part of a family relationship: to identify himself with the husband whom he half-wishes to supplant. Part of this same theme will be seen reversed when Charles meets Rodolphe after Emma's death:

> Charles se perdait en rêveries devant cette figure qu'elle avait aimée. Il lui semblait revoir quelque chose d'elle . . . Il aurait voulu être cet homme.

Rodolphe (see also pp. 23, 26, 31–35, 46–56, 71–72)

Léon sees himself as experiencing a romantic passion; Rodolphe sets out to seduce a woman and is coldly and clearly conscious of his aims and means. To obtain Emma is not even of vital importance in his life; after his fine battery of arguments at the agricultural show, six weeks go by; and if at first he remains away through technique, to provoke her impatience, afterwards it is because he has something better to do ('Il était parti pour la chasse'). He concludes without undue worry that it may be too late, but returns experimentally to see. Being less involved in feeling than Emma, he is ironically bound to retain the upper hand:

> avec cette supériorité de critique appartenant à celui qui, dans n'importe quel engagement, se tient en arrière.

Rodolphe might all too easily have appeared a mere villain and Flaubert's notes show him aware of this danger: 'Ne pas rendre Rodolphe

[1] See pp. 17, 53, 71.

odieux.' When he was sixteen, Flaubert had written a story, *Passion et Vertu*, in which a man of the world, after a cold estimate of the situation, set out to seduce a married woman:

> Il avait vu qu'elle aimait la poésie, la mer, le théâtre, Byron, et puis, résumant toutes ces observations en une seule, il avait dit: 'C'est une sotte, je l'aurai' (*Œuvres de Jeunesse*, I 243).

Rodolphe is his descendant, but something more subtle is made of him. His initial summing-up of prospects opens with

> Pauvre petite femme! Ça bâille après l'amour, comme une carpe après l'eau sur une table de cuisine.

—giving the superficial sympathy of the excuse that it will do her good, coupled with the scornful dehumanising 'ça', and the flatly true, devastatingly down-to-earth image. He goes on to enjoy the idea not just of physical conquest but of tenderness and charm; he ends with a clear consciousness of the complications of getting out of an affair when one has tired of it:

> Avec trois mots de galanterie, cela vous adorerait, j'en suis sûr! ce serait tendre! charmant! Oui, mais comment s'en débarrasser ensuite?

Rodolphe, with his 'bon sens bourgeois', finds Emma's sentimentality ridiculous, but her frank intensity flatters both 'son orgueil et sa sensualité'. In the contrast between him and Emma, Flaubert has shown at their extremes two conflicting attitudes to physical passion:

> ce qu'il ne comprenait pas, c'était tout ce trouble dans une chose aussi simple que l'amour—

why need pleasure entail these clinging demands and emotional intensities?

He leaves her firmly—yet not without feeling. As he sees her across the river on the last night:

> il fut pris d'un tel battement de cœur, qu'il s'appuya contre un arbre pour ne pas tomber.

For a moment both sensuality and tenderness conflict with commonsense and exasperation (how could he have wandered abroad, saddled with Emma and her child?), to end in 'Quel imbécile je suis . . . cela eût été trop bête.'

He goes home to sift idly through his pile of undifferentiated and forgotten love-letters, and to write to Emma. The letter breaking with her, like his first speeches of seduction, makes use of every device of high-flown romanticism—angels dragged into the abyss, thrones and talismans, the prayers of a child. These are directed to Emma's particular nature; the more general irony lies in the fact that the man who wishes to leave a woman and cannot force on her the bare truth will find his best excuse in the themes used here: the desire not to harm her, the dangers of loving too much, vague hope that one day they may meet again as calm friends.

Having written, he feels a moment of pity. The artificial tear he drops on the letter from a glass of water is at the same time a biting parody of what romanticism would require and a suggestion of something more serious: he who had mocked at the grandiose phrase 'n'accusez que la fatalité' from his letter yet lightly asserts that he cannot help his own nature: 'Mais, moi, je ne peux pas pleurer; ce n'est pas ma faute.'

When at the end of the book (III 8) Rodolphe tells Emma that he has not the money to give her, Flaubert stresses that 'il ne mentait point'. He could obtain it but will not make the effort, and the reasons are made clear. Emma's beauty and tears roused a moment of passion and tenderness; it is as he exclaims 'Pardonne-moi! J'ai été imbécile et méchant! Je t'aime, je t'aimerai toujours!' that he is suddenly met by her demand for money. Unable to see that in her muddled mental world money is utterly subsidiary to emotion, and himself taking for granted a stereotyped separation between 'passion' and 'prostitution', he concludes with a sense of cold shock that she had only one reason in coming. Emma puts the seal on his disillusion when she bursts out with the reproach, showing that he was not her only lover, 'tu ne vaux pas mieux que les autres'. And Flaubert adds the dry general reflection on how a demand for money can make the most icy interruption to a love-affair.

Rodolphe, then, is certainly not without feeling—but its range is limited, superficial and conventional, and this protects him; he smokes three pipes then goes to bed after leaving Emma, and sleeps peacefully on the night of her funeral. He who affects to despise the conventions has always been governed by them—in his disguised pride in being a notability at the *Comices*, or his dislike of receiving presents from a woman. We see him in one last stereotyped attitude; when Charles, after a struggle, refuses to blame him, Rodolphe considers that the Deceived Husband should have a different reaction, and looks on Charles as 'comique . . . et un peu vil'.

Charles (see also pp. 15–16, 25–26, 32–36, 50, 55, 67, 72)

The deceived husband was mocked at in comic tradition; a noble husband seen as the victim of an adulteress might have appealed to the sentimental. Charles as Flaubert creates him allows neither simple reaction. Probably no character has ever shown such an infuriating mixture of utter goodwill and total mediocrity. At school, where he symbolically starts in a daze of misunderstanding, having to write out the conjugation of the verb *ridiculus sum*, he is the conscientious nonentity, 'naturellement paisible'. Quite at sea in his medical studies he turns to petty dissipations, then manages to struggle his way through by sheer application. He is manœuvred by his mother, his first wife, Emma and Homais in turn. He is not even bold enough to ask Emma's father directly if he may marry her. It is he who persuades Emma to go riding with Rodolphe (even to writing that 'sa femme était à sa disposition') and to stay in Rouen to go to the Opera with Léon. He beatifically and ironically interprets her every gesture of exasperation or pretence as a sign of her loving care for himself. He bungles the operation on Hippolyte, and when Emma is poisoned is completely helpless, beseeching anyone and everyone to take some action.

Charles is incapable of looking into himself or others; in the early stages 'il ne chercha point à se demander pourquoi il venait aux Bertaux avec plaisir' and to the end he 'n'était pas de ceux qui descendent au fond des choses'. He does not even take part in the symphony of *idées reçues*; he lacks the bland certainty and the self-conscious effort to be superior. He is unimaginative and unenterprising, dreary in conversation, insupportably clumsy in gestures and mannerisms. Even his delight in becoming a father, contrasted with Emma's basic lack of interest in motherhood, is used to satirise in a suggestive image the human tendency to think that to breed, simply to hand on life, is the answer to all problems:

L'idée d'avoir engendré le délectait. Rien ne lui manquait à present. Il connaissait l'existence humaine tout du long, et s'y attablait sur les deux coudes avec sérénité (II 3).

Yet we are made to understand the detailed pleasures of his disorganised country upbringing, as he helps with the harvest, plays hopscotch in the Church porch on wet days, swings on the bell-rope, or watches the moths round the curé's candle on a summer evening, and his vague longings for the air and the smells of the country when he is pent up in a narrow street in Rouen. His marvelling joy in Emma is brought alive in the searching delight with which in the early mornings he gazes into the subtle shades and reflections in the depths of her eyes. He even has his brief moments of decisiveness (defending his first wife to his parents) or dream (the simple details he plans for the future of the child Berthe, as Emma lies beside him imagining a highly-coloured elopement). During Emma's nervous collapse he tends her devotedly for forty days, and his care for the child is seen in tiny details as he plants privet-sprigs for toy trees or makes rivers with the watering-can. Yet his plans are impractical and the child can learn nothing. His whole life is summed up by the puzzled phrase when Emma is dying: 'Est-ce ma faute? J'ai fait tout ce que j'ai pu, pourtant!', as in powerlessness and grief 'il la regardait avec des yeux d'une tendresse comme elle n'en avait jamais vu'.

The shock of her death works an ironical change in him. He, who let others organise everything, now writes instructions for her funeral beginning 'Je veux que . . .' and ending 'Je le veux. Faites-le.' He who was so prosaic makes the trappings elaborate and exaggerated, and afterwards takes on her own fashionable and feckless affectations and extravagances. When at last, having pushed aside the realisation as long as he can, he discovers her infidelities, he is completely demolished. In his last meeting with Rodolphe three feelings struggle: the desire to grasp at the memory of Emma through the man she had loved, the sudden surge of physical jealousy, and the dull fall into that weary and unquestioning resignation that reflects his basic nature, as he speaks 'd'une voix éteinte et avec l'accent résigné des douleurs infinies'.

Homais (see also pp. 16–17, 29–30, 34–37, 73–76, 78)

The bourgeois parades through nineteenth-century literature, displaying his stock beliefs and idiocies in Monnier's Joseph Prudhomme, or his ruthless progress upwards through society in the magnificent regiment of social thrusters created by Balzac, with Crevel foremost among them. Of them all it is Homais whose name has most firmly become a household word.

He is the epitome of bland complacency. Like Emma, he poses before the mirror of self-esteem; but where Emma cultivated a false ideal of the emotions, Homais displays the false stereotype of the intellect. On every issue from jam-making to the existence of God this busybody knows the answer, and knows it with condescending certainty.

In his correspondence, Flaubert wrote with disgust of how 'ce qui

devrait être étudié est cru sans discussion. Au lieu de regarder, on affirme.'
To Homais it is the high-sounding theories that matter, not their pains-
taking application in real life; as he says scornfully to Mme Lefrançois:

Croyez-vous qu'il faille, pour être agronome, avoir soi-même labouré
la terre ou engraissé des volailles?

The disastrous result of this gap between theory and practice, as of the
passion for over-simplified or conflicting theories (many of his disserta-
tions herald *Bouvard et Pécuchet*) appears in the operation on the club-foot
or in his treatment of the blind beggar. But the result is disastrous only to
others; when it comes to his own affairs Homais proceeds with caution.

Through him three important tendencies of nineteenth-century France
are satirised in the extremes to which they lead when misapplied by the
second-rate and second-hand mind: anti-clericalism, crude belief in 'progress', and the glorification of the family as a moral unit, which so easily
becomes the stifling conventionalism and ruthless self-seeking of the
closed family group. His sweeping theories are rendered ridiculous not
only by their superficiality, but by the incongruity of his indiscriminate
admirations:

J'ai moi-même . . . une bibliothèque composée des meilleurs auteurs:
Voltaire, Rousseau, Delille, Walter Scott, *L'Echo des feuilletons* . . .

But, with all his conventional ideas, the bourgeois likes to think of
himself as broad-minded, a bit of a gay dog. Towards the end, with
changing fashions, Homais

donnait maintenant dans un genre folâtre et parisien qu'il trouvait du
meilleur goût . . . même il parlait argot afin d'éblouir les bourgeois . . .
Il affectait le *genre artiste*, il fumait. Il s'acheta deux statuettes *chic*
Pompadour pour décorer son salon.

While protecting his family's morals with outraged dignity (just suppose
Athalie had found Justin's little book on sex!) he has always enjoyed a
salacious conversation in the 'right' company and is constantly digging
Léon in the ribs with allusions to a young man's follies: he is the bourgeois
stereotype of 'l'esprit gaulois'.

Under the bluster and good-fellowship lies cowardice. He is afraid of
the authorities, who may prosecute him for illegal prescribing; his hatred
of the priest is the result of his unconscious fear of death; he shudders at
the sight of his own blood. His complacency and cowardice reach their

heights during and after Emma's death. It is in the detail of his beliefs, his conversation, his manœuvres and his newspaper articles that we find a magnificent compendium of bourgeois behaviour. He attains superb stature as a comic figure.[1]

At the end of the book, he who had prided himself on being the follower of the 'immortels principes de 89' goes over to the Monarchy, sends a flattering petition to the King, and is decorated. Flaubert had at one time planned another end: he imagined Homais puffed up in a paroxysm of pride and flaunting his decoration before rows of mirrors; suddenly everything seems to turn in a dizzy whirl and the most terrible of doubts overcomes him as he, the victor in the real world, wonders whether he is real at all, or simply a figment of the imagination invented by some ridiculous author. This delight in playing with different angles of vision on how the artist creates his illusion, and disrupting that illusion by sudden shifts of viewpoint within the work itself, has intrigued original and experimental artists from Furetière's *Roman Bourgeois* or Corneille's *Illusion comique* to Gide's *Faux-Monnayeurs* and beyond. Here such an end would have introduced a fantastic note too sudden to fit the tone of the rest of the novel (moreover, to make Homais doubt himself would be to destroy his bland and gigantic charlatanism), and Flaubert rightly rejected it. Yet one still rejoices in the idea of Homais left to face his own image at last.

4. *Values*

Voir les choses en farce est le seul moyen de ne pas les voir en noir.
(*Corr.* II 472)

. . . Je ne sais quelle sensibilité profonde et cachée.
(*Corr. Supp.* IV 318)

Characters who at the same time so closely echo and parody cherished human reactions have left some readers with a feeling of the author's uncompromising bitterness. Flaubert has been spoken of as a great artist whose work yet lacks human sympathy, or a sense of the dignity and value of life. This kind of distinction may perhaps unfairly but irresistibly

[1] See below, pp. 73–75.

recall his own picture of Homais the critic, airing contradictory views on *Athalie*:

> De cette tragédie, il blâmait les idées, mais il admirait le style; il maudissait la conception, mais il applaudissait à tous les details, et s'exaspérait contre les personnages, en s'enthousiasmant de leurs discours . . . et dans cette confusion de sentiments où il s'embarrassait, il aurait voulu tout à la fois pouvoir couronner Racine de ses deux mains et discuter avec lui pendant un bon quart d'heure (II 3).

Of course, Flaubert has created a selective, heightened and personal vision of things, and his readers are bound to set it against other ways of looking at life. He has often been compared, for example, with Tolstoy or Hardy, who convey very differently human tenderness and human majesty. He himself sardonically remarked on the tendency of critics to look for oranges on apple trees; his own admiration for the authors he found great was expansive and generous. Many readers will fortunately be able to take for granted that a bitter vision of life may have its own tonic values, may show the power of the human mind to face, shape and express what is most disturbing in human experience. But also, Flaubert is far from reducing humanity to petty insignificance. He conveys an original stature and value even through what he ruthlessly criticizes or pitilessly deflates.

He himself often remarked on how he deliberately directed critical laughter even at those things which seemed to him to matter most. This he certainly does. To a writer who has despaired of all other absolutes, particularly in the nineteenth century, there will often be a strong temptation to present Art as the one true value; Flaubert has caricatured even this in the figure of Binet sitting apart in the peaceful absorption of meticulous artifice. But to probe into the dangers inherent in vital qualities, to set going conflicting reflections around possible values, is no mere nihilism. Flaubert's searing mockery comes back to a positive implication:

> Il n'est pas de choses, faits, sentiments ou gens, sur lesquels je n'aie passé naïvement ma bouffonnerie, comme un rouleau de fer à lustrer les pièces d'étoffes. C'est une bonne méthode. On voit ensuite ce qui en reste. Il est trois fois enraciné dans vous le sentiment que vous y laissez, en plein vent, sans tuteur ni fil de fer, et débarrassé de toutes ces convenances si utiles . . . Il est bon et il peut même être beau de rire de la vie, pourvu qu'on vive (*Corr.* II 378).

E

This is not drab desperation, but an assertion of positive values in the critical comic vision and in the sheer experience of life.

Obviously intentions are not necessarily the same as results, but it is worth recalling some of Flaubert's intentions. It is easy to quote from the correspondence his frequent expressions of disgust and hatred at the spectacle of the human condition. Letters are of course a safety-valve for violent exasperation, and there are other moments to be seen. When he was planning *L'Education sentimentale*, he wrote to George Sand:

> Je ne veux avoir ni amour, ni haine, ni pitié, ni colère. Quant à de la sympathie, c'est différent: jamais on n'en a assez (*Corr.* V 397).

Sympathy as he sees it should be adulterated by neither admiration nor condescension, but show a detached and imaginative understanding. After reading *Uncle Tom's Cabin* he remarked:

> Je n'ai pas besoin, pour m'attendrir sur un esclave que l'on torture, que cet esclave soit brave homme, bon père, bon époux et chante des hymnes . . . (*Corr.* III 60).

Sympathy for a noble victim may easily become smug and sentimental, whereas the capacity to understand something less appealing has a different value.

> Non, nous ne sommes pas bons, mais cette faculté de s'assimiler à toutes les misères et de se supposer les ayant est peut-être la vraie charité humaine (*Corr.* III 225).

All-embracing sympathy of this kind may sometimes be the outcome of a grim vision of man's condition. It has also been suggested that it would logically lead to an undifferentiated world in which no scale of importance is possible. It is perhaps the very strength of the two urges in Flaubert—to demolish critically and to share imaginatively—that prevents his implying the logical extremes of hatred or indifference sometimes attributed to him. He gives us not the philosopher's abstraction, but the artist's creation.

'Toutes les misères': the phrase may suggest that he is concerned with pathos rather than grandeur. If on the one hand he does not want to associate sympathy with facile admiration, on the other he does not wish to make it a matter of easy pity. Perhaps one of the most suggestive observations he made was: 'l'esprit tendre, le cœur âpre'. He is aware, like La Rochefoucauld before him, of the dangers of pity as an emotional indulgence, a disguised form of self-regard. So those characters who are victims, likely to provoke an over-automatic reaction, are deliberately set at a distance and deprived of any spurious appeal. The work-worn hands of Catherine Leroux are movingly described (II 8)—scrubbed clean, but chafed and discoloured by years of dust from the barns, chemicals from the washing and grease from the wool, they hang half-open 'comme pour présenter d'elles-mêmes l'humble témoignage de tant de souffrances subies'; but she herself is shown as reduced to a kind of dazed stupor, quite unaware of her own wretchedness:

> Rien de triste ou d'attendri n'amollissait ce regard pâle. Dans la fréquentation des animaux, elle avait pris leur mutisme et leur placidité.

Yet beneath petty events and deficiencies of character two kinds of implication may be seen. In earlier versions, Flaubert had directly analysed both the qualities and the defects in Charles' mother: 'Sa passion pour Charles avait . . . ce caractère caressant et pédagogique à la fois des passions des vieillards, absorption finale, qui condensant l'individu le résument avec ses énergies variées, contradictoires, *égoisme, dévouement, abnégation et despotisme.*' In the book these are suggested by her words, actions and thoughts. In her misery at being neglected after her son's marriage, she is shown in the sharp image of someone who peers through the window of what was once her house and watches strangers comfortably installed at table there (I 7). Later, when her husband dies, she sits stitching at her black clothes, with the tears dripping grotesquely along her nose as

> les pires jours d'autrefois lui réapparaissaient enviables. Tout s'effaçait sous le regret instinctif d'une si longue habitude (III 2).

The sentiment is not idealised—there is a deliberate twist of irony—but an insight into a basic experience is conveyed. It is the same when Charles hears of his father's death and is made aware of a latent feeling as he

> s'étonnait de sentir tant d'affection pour cet homme qu'il avait cru jusqu'alors n'aimer que très médiocrement,

and there follows, in its useless and flat bareness, the automatic human desire: 'J'aurais voulu le revoir encore.'

Emma's father too remembers the past as he returns from his daughter's wedding (I 4); he thinks of the first ride home with his young wife on the crupper of his horse, the basket she was carrying, the lace strings of her bonnet twisting in the wind, her cold fingers that she warmed against him. Here, it is a genuine delight that is remembered, but again the mood is deliberately removed from sentimentality: his mind is still hazy from drinks at the wedding; he thinks of paying a visit to the churchyard but is afraid of increasing his sorrow, so shrugs it off as best he may and goes home. It was he who, in his attempted consolation to Charles at the death of Charles' first wife, gave in fumbling, colloquial form the outline of human grief with its desperation, gradual acceptance, lasting weight of loss, knowledge of necessity, and sense that life goes on:

> Quand j'ai eu perdu ma pauvre défunte . . . j'aurais voulu être . . . crevé. Eh bien, tout doucement, un jour chassant l'autre, ça a coulé brin à brin, miette à miette; ça s'en est allé, . . . c'est descendu, je veux dire, car il vous reste toujours quelque chose au fond comme qui dirait . . . un poids, là, sur la poitrine! Mais puisque c'est notre sort à tous . . . Il faut vous secouer, Monsieur Bovary . . . (I 3).

These minor characters show the ironies behind human feeling, and they are often grotesque or inarticulate in their expression. To Flaubert 'L'ironie n'enlève rien au pathétique, elle l'outre au contraire' (*Corr.* III 43).

And sometimes they are briefly made to suggest what may appear a negative quality, but is one of the most vital: unpretentiousness. Of the letter from Charles' mother telling him of her husband's death, Flaubert has in passing used one of his most significant phrases: she recounted it 'sans aucune hypocrisie sentimentale'.[1] A quality of the same kind, again conveyed only obliquely, is disinterestedness: the absence of the profiteering instinct, the delight in a thing simply for its own sake. Something of this is outlined in Justin's devotion to Emma without thought of fulfilment. In earlier versions it was commented on in the abstract; in the final novel we have simply his actions, and the image that gives a moment of

---

[1] In the correspondence (III 105) Flaubert says of the young Crépet: 'il cherche (*mais naïvement et sans pose, conséquemment c'est respectable*) un idéal'. Madame Arnoux in *L'Education sentimentale* has unpretentiousness as her basic characteristic: 'Elle répondit sans aucune exagération de bêtise maternelle'; 'Elle ne s'exaltait point pour la littérature mais son esprit charmait par des mots simples et pénétrants.' A quality given positive form in the later novel is suggested only obliquely in *Madame Bovary*. It will lead to Félicité in *Un Cœur Simple*: 'devouée sans exaltation . . .'

strong sympathy at the end: 'un enfant pleurait . . . sous la pression d'un regret immense, plus doux que la lune et plus insondable que la nuit'.[1]

One scene as a whole is essential to the impression left on the mind by Flaubert's characters. He writes of Emma's death in one of his letters (III 344), saying first that it will not provoke the same kind of tears as the fate of the innocent heroine of *Paul et Virginie*, then that the reader will surely feel for Charles, and finally that the centre is to be the fact and implications of death itself. He had also written that 'il faut que mon bon-homme vous émeuve pour tous les veufs'. 'Mon bonhomme'—behind the frightened ineptitude and, later, wild manifestations of grief in that mediocre individual Charles Bovary, Flaubert conveys his genuine tenderness and genuine anguish—but above all the conflict of feelings in anyone who faces death and loss. We follow through the effort to prevent the end, the silent waiting, the grip on hands in a physical attempt to hold back the dying, the hypnotic sound of prayers set against the last convulsions, then, when death has to be faced, the outburst of revolt, the thought that the body will become one with the physical loveliness of the universe, the sudden horror of the facts of decay, the memories of both the most vital and the most trivial moments from the past (their wedding, and a place where they happened one day to sit in the Church), the sheer strain of the last services, earth falling on coffin with 'ce bruit formidable qui nous semble être le retentissement de l'éternité', and finally the bitter but authentic notation when the stress of prolonged obligatory ceremony ends with 'la vague satisfaction d'en avoir fini'. Even to pick out these points is to falsify Flaubert's effect; they must be set in their context of trivial detail, against the background of continuing life, with the Homais family in a fluster trying to impress the great surgeon at dinner and the village crowding in for free consultations, if we are to see how human sympathy in Flaubert is the more intense for being utterly uninflated.

As for Emma in this scene, Flaubert has spared her nothing. In the magnificently constructed sentence evoking the priest's gestures of ex-treme unction over each part of her body, he concentrates deliberately on the memory of her lusts and her luxuries, her pride and her pretences. The past called up is that of Emma Bovary: the tone has deliberately the

[1] Justin's is an instinctive passion without deforming self-consciousness; the early Léon suggests the theme that will be taken up in Frédéric's love for Mme Arnoux in *L'Education sentimentale*, involving both worship and escapism, cowardice and genuine self-sacrifice.

resonance of Bossuet. The richly balanced sentences evoke at the same time the life of an individual and the dignity of an age-long ritual; the last phrases rise to echo in sound and rhythm the urgency and intensity of her life, then fall into nothingness

> enfin sur la plante des pieds, si rapides autrefois quand elle courait à l'assouvissance de ses desirs, et qui maintenant ne marcheraient plus.

The whole movement suggests not only the pathos but the strange majesty in frail and fallible human existence as it struggles, enjoys, sins, suffers and disappears.

But imaginative insight is not confined to suffering. When Flaubert writes of what he felt as the creator of one of the scenes between Emma and Rodolphe, the passage suggests also how it will involve the reader:

> Aujourd'hui, homme et femme tout ensemble, amant et maîtresse à la fois, je me suis promené à cheval dans une forêt, par un après-midi d'automne, sous des feuilles jaunes, et j'étais les chevaux, les feuilles, le vent, les paroles qu'ils se disaient et le soleil rouge qui faisait s'entre-fermer leurs paupières (*Corr.* III 405).

It has been suggested that the beauty of the outer world is seen through the eyes of the artist, not through those of characters who may be too limited to appreciate it. Certainly Flaubert shows how, when they remember their past, loss and memory make them attribute to it an impression of delight and beauty which at the time they did not consciously experience, as when Emma thinks back to her youth on the farm. Yet in these moments, tiny sense-impressions in the present are given a particular evocative value as they suddenly recall the sharp loveliness and worth of an everyday world which the characters in their questing appetites and emotional careerism had ignored or scorned. Emma suddenly sees the grey flakes of ash used to dry the ink on a letter from her father; they make her think of him bending to pick up the tongs by the hearth and so remember how she would hold a stick to burn and spark in the flame or sunlit summer evenings when

> quelquefois les abeilles, tournoyant dans la lumière, frappaient contre les carreaux comme des balles d'or rebondissantes (II 10).

Emma could not herself express her feeling in these precise and suggestive words; and there is an ironical contrast between the past as she now sees it and her boredom when it was real, but Flaubert has conveyed a vital part of her experience which she herself misrepresents, ignores, or cannot formulate.

Often, intent on their dream, the characters 'ne voient pas le beau où il se trouve'—the beauty that lies so unexpectedly in the smallest details of the ordinary world, as in the docks of Rouen or the garden at Tostes where Emma feels only stifling monotony, yet

> la rosée avait laissé sur les choux des guipures d'argent avec de longs fils clairs qui s'étendaient de l'un à l'autre (I 9).

But these details, even when the characters are only half-conscious of them, make the substance of their lives and create the particular atmosphere behind what will stand in their memory. Emma and Léon walk together by the river (II 3)—their conscious attention is focused on discussing Spanish dancers in Rouen; at an unconscious level they are being intensely drawn towards each other. Meantime the sense of warm promise and obscure threat that is growing in them is conveyed through the detailed suggestions in sights and sensations of which they are only half-aware—the sun-warmed garden walls topped with broken bottles, the river with its trailing water-weeds, slender-legged insects and tiny blue bubbles endlessly circling and bursting, Emma's sunshade striking clouds of yellow dusty pollen from the wallflowers, or its silk caught by trailing honeysuckle. Even if they can neither analyse nor express all this, it is a part of their being. And through it Flaubert has given us a heightened apprehension of the real world, of their feelings, and of the patterns of analogy implicit in these slightest details.

Sometimes they are aware of beauty but cannot express it, as with Rodolphe's bare, inadequate comment during the last evening (II 12) by the river: 'Ah! la belle nuit!' Here we come to the crux of what Flaubert suggests through his characters: so important that he intervenes with a more developed direct comment than anywhere else in the book.

When Emma pours out to Rodolphe her jealousy and her devotion, he has so often heard these same words from other women that he seems to face in its bare dullness 'l'éternelle monotonie de la passion, qui a toujours les mêmes formes et le même langage'. But he is mistaken. Flaubert's first comment is:

> Il ne distinguait pas, cet homme si plein de pratique, la dissemblance des sentiments sous la parité des expressions (II 12).

One of the most deeply-rooted human experiences is to be conscious that our feelings and our words follow patterns endlessly repeated throughout the ages, and yet to feel ineradicably that in each individual experience there is something new, sharp, individual to be communicated, if only words could be found to express its unique quality. If one side of Flaubert's technique is ruthlessly to reduce human behaviour to the lowest common denominator of 'l'éternelle lamentation', the other is to suggest the irreducible individuality that lies behind it. From his adolescent work on Don Juan ('C'est pourtant toujours la même chose, dit Leporello—Eh! non, ce n'est jamais la même chose') to the late letters to Maupassant, he comes constantly back to the sense of individual and relative values beneath the outer monotony of experience or triteness of expression.

Rodolphe takes for granted that Emma's affected clichés prove only mediocrity and pretence; Flaubert, who spares her no criticism, yet makes clear that he is wrong: beneath inadequate words may lie genuine needs, longings and sufferings:

> Comme si la plénitude de l'âme ne débordait pas quelquefois par les métaphores les plus vides, puisque personne, jamais, ne peut donner l'exacte mesure de ses besoins, ni de ses conceptions, ni de ses douleurs, et que la parole humaine est comme un chaudron fêlé où nous battons des mélodies à faire danser les ours, quand on voudrait attendrir les étoiles (II 12).

The unimaginative Rodolphe misinterprets both Emma and Charles. When at the end of the book he scorns Charles for not hating his wife's lover, Flaubert had originally made the direct comment:

> Car il ne comprenait rien à . . . la passion vide d'orgueil, sans respect humain, ni conscience, qui plonge tout entière dans l'être aimé . . . et touche presque aux proportions d'une idée pure, à force de largeur et d'impersonnalité (P.L. 641).

For by the side of those who manœuvre successfully in the practical world, there is another dimension of dramatic dignity in both Emma and Charles, each of whom pushes to distorted extremes a quality which might have been great, and each of whom genuinely and intensely suffers. In a letter Flaubert wrote:

> La contemplation d'une existence rendue misérable par une passion violente, de quelque nature qu'elle soit, est toujours quelque chose d'instructif et de hautement moral. Ça rabaisse . . . tant de passions

banales et de manies vulgaires que l'on est satisfait en songeant que l'instrument humain peut vibrer jusque là (*Corr.* II 32).

It is not that intensity and suffering are made (as is the temptation with the romantics) automatic criteria of value. Questions of worth in Flaubert are suggested by ironical interplay between the characters and not seen in unadulterated form in one individual. Two qualities he deliberately does not allow his main figures: intellectual and aesthetic discrimination. Yet these are precisely the values that are most implicit in the book, in what it requires of the reader if he is to share its irony, its tragedy and its comedy.

The sense of comedy is certainly one of the tonic values in *Madame Bovary*: a particular kind of conquest by both intellect and instinct over the unsatisfactory nature of things. The comic vision at its heights implies a capacity to stand detached for a moment from the emotional reactions of anger or pity (which may still underlie or follow it) and grasp, whether in an instinctive flash or through conscious analysis, the exasperating and stimulating patterns of incongruity in events, men or things. Flaubert once wrote of *le rire* as 'la plus haute manière de voir la vie'. Once again, he saw it as a two-sided quality: 'le dédain et la compréhension mêlés' (*Corr.* IV 33).

His sense of incongruity tends of course to the bitter, the ironical and the satirical, and often he sets his humour against a grim background. But when Homais has been asked to break gently to Emma the news of her father-in-law's death, there is a finely developed comic contrast as he, who has prepared a rounded, polished, rhythmical speech, prudent, delicate and full of skilled gradations, is so roused to pompous wrath by Justin's lack of respect for the poison cupboard that he keeps Emma standing in suspense while he hurls at the boy an interminable flood of inaptly rhetorical rebuke ('Il citait du latin, tant il était exaspéré. Il eût cité du chinois et du groënlandais, s'il eût connu ces deux langues'), and when finally brought down to earth can only blurt out 'Votre beau-père est mort.'

Round this central contrast Flaubert has grouped the revealing and creative comic detail. In one tiny incident he brings alive with a sharp savour, set in the ceremonial of the annual jam-making, Homais' pomposity, his overbearing treatment of Justin, his pride in being responsible for Matters of Life and Death, his terror at the danger of being poisoned,

and a great deal more. The comic is often founded on a particular com-
bination of the expected and the unexpected: we see a man prove
mechanically and infallibly true to type, but in an elaboration of imaginative detail that we could neither foresee nor ourselves invent. Homais
certainly provides this delight. We know him to be anti-clerical: we
watch him with fiendish ingenuity force the tiniest detail of Bournisien's
behaviour into his stereotyped conceptions—if the priest politely refuses
a drink this is sure proof of clerical hypocrisy, since it is common know-
ledge that all priests tipple in secret; if he helps with the haymaking it is
because he has the vigorous physique of a dangerous seducer. There is a
comic clash between the grandiose build-up of the Vices of the Clergy
and the cheerful, inept Bournisien as he is; between the vocabulary of
condescendingly colloquial opening ('les prêtres godaillaient', 'des
gaillards pareils') and of inappositely oratorical peroration:

> ce qui nous démontre, en passant, que les prêtres ont toujours croupi
> dans une ignorance turpide, où ils s'efforcent d'engloutir avec eux
> les populations. Il se tut, cherchant des yeux un public autour de
> lui, car, dans son effervescence, le pharmacien, un moment, s'était
> cru en plein conseil municipal (II 1).

His newspaper articles make of the clumsy scenes of the agricultural show
a lofty mixture of military epic and sentimental pastoral, and transform
the damp squibs of the fireworks out of all recognition:

> Le soir, un brillant feu d'artifice a tout à coup illuminé les airs. On eût
> dit un véritable kaléidoscope, un vrai décor d'Opéra, et, un moment,
> notre petite localité a pu se croire transportée au milieu d'un rêve des
> *Mille et une Nuits* (II 8).

At the end, this representative of modern science becomes the great
introducer of *le cho-ca* into the region, and we have the spectacle of his
adoring wife lost in admiration at the sight of the Pulvermacher hydro-
electric chain worn for his health under his flannel waistcoat:

> Madame Homais restait tout éblouie devant la spirale d'or sous laquelle
> il disparaissait, et sentait redoubler ses ardeurs pour cet homme plus
> garrotté qu'un Scythe et splendide comme un mage (III 11).

Finally it is he who fittingly invents a ridiculous and ironical Latin
epitaph for Emma. In fact, Homais, that prosaic and sinister phenomenon,

takes on through creative elaboration a kind of epic stature and poetic absurdity.

But delight in the detail of pure comedy is not confined to the more obviously comic characters. Emma and Léon are one day conducting a conversation on disillusion: wanting either to provoke his jealousy or to share part of the truth, she tells him that she once loved someone else. Hastily she adds that of course it was platonic. The moment of sheer comedy comes as Léon asks for details and Emma immediately invents: 'Il était capitaine de vaisseau, mon ami.' The invention is both logical and gloriously incongruous—logical because Léon cannot set out to pursue such an elusive figure, and should admire her for having been loved by the type of the bellicose and romantic male; incongruous as we see Rodolphe transformed into such terms, and listen to the tranquil 'mon ami' with which she imparts this piece of sublime misinformation.

The *idée reçue* is obviously a source of comedy, and Flaubert will sometimes push it to its deliberate *reductio ad absurdum* in imaginative illustration. Stories of the lost dog who returns home are a source of perennial wonder: Emma's greyhound (in the early stages her substitute for a *confidant*, alternately envied because it cannot suffer and credited with human sympathies) disappears, and Lheureux has a consoling set of tales where a slow series of authenticating details ('cinquante lieues, quatre rivières, un caniche, son père, un soir, comme il allait dîner en ville') and the sweep of fantasy ('un chien qui était revenu de Constantinople à Paris') produce a new comic version of the legend.

Objects too may show fine comic discrepancies. In the tympanum of the imitation Greek temple which is the town-hall of Yonville stands a symbolic carving: 'un coq gaulois, appuyé d'une patte sur la Charte et tenant de l'autre les balances de la justice'. Or we remember the virtuoso piece describing the sentimental gallimaufry that tops the culinary *pièce de résistance* at Emma's wedding. Flaubert cut out of the novel in its final form the ridiculously decorated silk scarf belonging to the maid and the educational toy given to the Homais children; he was obviously anxious not to overload the book with set-pieces, but we may still regret the removal of these signs of his sheer joy in the reflections provoked by the crazy results of human ingenuity.

One character is often treated as an exception by Flaubert's critics: the doctor Larivière. Certainly Flaubert does not direct against him the same kind of irony as he applies to his other characters. The biographical explanation—that he is giving a portrait of his father—whether or not it is true, is insufficient. Larivière might be set in a line that runs from Balzac's Bianchon to Camus' Rieux—the man who in face of social or metaphysical complexities is well aware that he can provide no abstract or absolute solution, but directs both clear intelligence and deep feeling to making what he can of circumstances as they are.

He, unlike other characters, has penetrating intelligence. And that intelligence is ruthless in stripping away pretence and affectation:

> Son regard, plus tranchant que ses bistouris, vous descendait droit dans l'âme et désarticulait tout mensonge à travers les allégations et les pudeurs (III 8).

He sweeps aside the elaborations of Homais who is portentously explaining his skilled scientific efforts ('*primo*, j'ai délicatement introduit dans un tube') with the crude, practical, down-to-earth 'Il aurait mieux valu lui introduire vos doigts dans la gorge', and even enjoys a rough pun at the chemist's expense when asked about his blood-pressure: 'Oh! ce n'est pas le *sens* qui le gêne.' His uncompromising diagnoses and skill have saved others; for Emma there is nothing he can now do, and, finding himself powerless against the fact of death, he makes no pretence about it—'il n'y a plus rien à faire'—yet feels a deep pity for Charles.

Larivière in fact may serve as a symbol of the novelist and his art. The pitiless analysis of pretence, the amused and almost brutal mockery at pretentiousness, the pity for suffering, the firm sense of the insoluble problems of human life, the bending of all resources of feeling and intelligence to a particular task; these are the basic qualities. There is one central phrase: 'pratiquant la vertu sans y croire'. He refuses abstractions and absolutes, but in his harsh and loving contact with the immediate detail of human existence his art exercises its vital value. With the same qualities and the same refusals, Flaubert may both destroy the falsities and suggest something of the ineradicable worth of human life behind the weaknesses of individuals or the paradoxes of theoretical problems.

Certainly Flaubert has set at odds the hankerings, submissions, self-seekings and self-satisfactions of the human race, and made of them a probing and uncomfortable instrument for analysing both ourselves and the nature of things. His characters are rarely allowed to combine for long those qualities that through interplay and implication may be suggested as potential values: intelligence, sensibility, unpretentiousness, disinterestedness. And each of these values is unremittingly accompanied by its concomitant exaggeration or paradox. Aspiration may be prolonged into greed, bitterness or fruitless day-dream; acceptance become unreflecting and spineless; the artifice and hypocrisy of self-consciousness play against the dull absence of conscious reflection or the clear-minded and unimaginative careerism. We are faced with the ambiguity of all human possibilities, and left to work out our personal response. This we can do only if we have fully shared the detailed experiences of the characters, with their conflicting stimulus to sensations, emotions, intellectual or moral concepts. Any discussion of what they stand for will always be over-simplified, this brief study in particular. What we shall come back to with renewed delight is the way Flaubert creates in detail the rich illusion of life. And this in turn depends on control over words: words which if applied loosely or complacently may reduce the truest observation to vague or slick superficiality, but here are used precisely and suggestively to sharpen all our perceptions and make of the slightest experience a source of prolonged and subtle satisfaction.

It is through the shape of her nails, the pricks on her fingers as she tries practical sewing in emergency, her gesture as she stands with head thrown back, licking the last drops from the liqueur glass, that Emma's nature is suggested to us before we know anything abstract about her. The sense of Charles' growing love is evoked without comment in a scene of momentary poised beauty as, on a day of melting snow, she stands beneath her sunshade: the wind ruffling the soft hairs on the nape of her neck and twisting her apron-strings evokes sensuous loveliness; the sun falling through the shot-silk gives a warm caress and a shifting uncertainty in the iridescent play of light, and there is the final slow, satisfying resonance as 'on entendait les gouttes d'eau, une à une, tomber sur la moire tendue' (I 2).

When Emma in the convent turns over the pages of the ridiculous and touching romantic albums that start her dreams—

> maniant délicatement leurs belles reliures de satin . . en soulevant de son haleine le papier de soie des gravures, qui se levait à demi plié et retombait doucement contre la page (I 6)

—we are set inside her experience by the delicate rendering of the caressing, diaphanous tissue-paper, so light that an eager breath disturbs it; while the sense of enchanting promise, to be followed by disillusion, is, in a different tone, very close to the opening of Baudelaire's *Le Voyage*, where the child pores over maps and prints by lamplight. And the lamp-shade of the convent dormitory, or that other lampshade she mechani-cally twists during the long evenings in Yonville, seem to point ahead to the shade that created a richer illusion for the child Marcel in *A la recherche du temps perdu*.

The order and ease of aristocratic life as she briefly sees it is summed up in the light, accurate click of billiard balls; its sensuous warmth and dimmed glitter in the crystals of the candelabra 'couverts d'une buée mate'. Her boredom is drawn with weary knife-lines on the waxcloth of the table-top; her apparent reconciliation with her mother-in-law is sealed with respectability when she humbly asks for a recipe for pickled gherkins. Her impatience on the weekly drive to Rouen comes alive as she unavailingly shuts her eyes to cheat herself over the exact sequence of fields, posts or huts; the temptation by Lheureux shimmers before her eyes as he flicks with his nail the spangled silks that rustle and glitter in the greenish light of a low room at evening. The Homais family reveals its essence when Justin is told to take the children for a walk because if they go to sleep in the armchairs they drag the loose covers out of place; the grief of Emma's father at her funeral is imprinted on the memory by the dye from his new smock that sets its stain among the tears and dust on his face.

Even the most prosaic detail of what people wear on their feet is made to fit their nature and moods: the stiff parallel ridges on country boots, the careful polishing by the meticulous Binet, the soft supple leather worn by Rodolphe, Emma's swansdown slippers. But hands are made par-ticularly expressive: Emma's, when we first see her, suggesting elegance and a certain insensitivity; the deliberate contrast in the moment when the rough hands of Catherine Leroux hang half-open in lifelong accep-tance, while Emma and Rodolphe, suddenly grasping at what they desire, intertwine their fingers; the many other occasions where words prove inadequate and hands grope after each other, with the underlying irony of how different may be the feelings of two human beings held in this physical contact; the hands of Emma on her deathbed ('ses pauvres mains . . . avec ce geste hideux et doux des agonisants'); or the hands of Larivière, always without gloves, ready to undertake the surgeon's grim and practical work.

For one thing was absent when Emma dreamed of total bliss with Rodolphe: since all was to be perfect, 'rien de particulier ne surgissait: les jours, tous magnifiques, se ressemblaient comme des flots'. By the side of this abstract ideal of perfection, the life of every day, petty, exasperating and unsatisfactory, has, for those who can see, the sharp individuality that gives significance to the tragic or the comic vision. Where plot or surface may most seem to suggest the futility of things, the underlying substance constantly brings us back to this source of delight, and to Flaubert's own remark: 'Aimez les faits pour eux-mêmes. La contemplation peut être pleine de tendresse.'

More than in any other novel, perhaps, the sense and the value of each detail depends on the repercussions of the whole, on its place in the 'harmonie de l'ensemble' which each reader will experience and judge for himself. Flaubert created a particularly solid and suggestive physical world; in it, through people, through things, and through their interrelationships he provoked conflicting reflections on the possibilities and limitations of the human condition. A phrase from a letter on the work of a novelist he admired might well sum up his own *Madame Bovary*: 'On voit et on rêve.'

Suggestions for Further Reading

Flaubert's works may be consulted in the Conard edition (including the *Oeuvres de Jeunesse*, nine volumes of *Correspondance* and a four-volume Supplement); more recent editions, of collective or separate works, include those of the Centenaire, Belles Lettres (Textes français), Pléiade, Intégrale. The Correspondence is now appearing in a revised and much amplified form, edited by J. Bruneau (Vol. I, Pléiade, 1973).

The most reliable text of *Madame Bovary* is that edited by C. Gothot-Mersch for the Classiques Garnier, 1971; this indicates important details where different editions contain errors as compared with Flaubert's final manuscript.

Students of this novel should specially enjoy consulting Flaubert's early plans, uninhibited comments, and long passages eventually cut out, as presented in *Madame Bovary, nouvelle version précédée des scénarios inédits*, ed. J. Pommier and G. Leleu, and *Ébauches et Fragments inédits*, ed. G. Leleu, 1936. C. Gothot-Mersch, in *La Genèse de 'Madame Bovary'*, 1966, gives a thorough and thoughtful study of the planning of the novel; cf. also the introduction to her edition (above), with its succinct conspectus of some main critical views.

General works on Flaubert in English vary considerably in quality. For links between novels and biography see the studies by P. Spencer, 1952, and E. Starkie, 2 vols., 1967 and 1972. For widely differing critical views, V. Brombert: *The novels of Flaubert*, 1966; J. Culler, *Flaubert. The uses of uncertainty*, 1974; R. J. Sherrington: *Three novels of Flaubert*, 1970; A. Thorlby: *Gustave Flaubert and the Art of Realism*, 1956; M. G. Tillett: *On Reading Flaubert*, 1961.

General studies in French have been many, from the early but still excellent *Gustave Flaubert* by A. Thibaudet (Gallimard, reprinted 1964) to the recent thorough and thoughtful *Flaubert* by Cl. Digeon (Hatier, 1970) or the stimulating *Flaubert par lui-même* by V. Brombert (Seuil, 1971). Digeon's book gives a specially good selected reading list, with brief critical comments. Cf. also P. Moreau's 'État présent des études flaubertiennes', in *L'information littéraire*, 1957, and C. B. West's 'Ten Years of Flaubert Studies', in *Modern Languages*, Sept. 1968. R. Debray-Genette provides extracts from some of the most interesting critics (Firmin-Didot, 1970).

For fuller references see the general bibliographies by Talvart and Place, Dreher and Rolli; the invaluable annual bibliographies by R. Rancoeur and by O. Klapp, also those of *The Year's Work in Modern Language Studies* and *Publications of the Modern Language Association of America*, and the periodical *Les Amis de Flaubert*. These will give details on standard scholarly and critical studies (e.g. those by G. Bollème, L. Bopp, J. Bruneau, S. Cigada, A. Cento, P. Danger, G. L. Demorest, R. Descharmes, R. Dumesnil, M. J. Durry, E. Ferrère, E. Maynial, M. Nadeau, J. Seznec, J. Suffel); on important comments by creative writers past and present (Baudelaire, Henry James, Proust, Valéry, J.-P. Sartre, Nathalie Sarraute); on stimulating chapters from books on general problems (e.g. works by Ch. Du Bos, P. Lubbock, E. Auerbach, G. Poulet, S. Ullmann, J.-P. Richard, R. Girard, G. Lukács, G. Genette, etc.); on many valuable articles in periodicals.

The above suggestions are necessarily selective. The reader of *Madame Bovary* may make many further discoveries among critical works, and still more discoveries each time he re-examines his own reactions on re-reading the book itself.